The Trans-Pacific Partnership and Asia-Pacific Integration:
A Quantitative Assessment

Peterson
Institute for
International
Economics

1750 Massachusetts Avenue, NW
Washington, DC 20036–1903
(202) 328-9000   Fax (202) 659-3225
www.piie.com

EAST-WEST
CENTER

1601 East-West Road
Honolulu, HI 96848-1601
(808) 944-7111   Fax (808) 944-7376
www.eastwestcenter.org

The Trans-Pacific Partnership and Asia-Pacific Integration: A Quantitative Assessment

Peter A. Petri, Michael G. Plummer, and Fan Zhai

PETERSON INSTITUTE FOR INTERNATIONAL ECONOMICS
EAST-WEST CENTER
Washington, DC | November 2012

Peter A. Petri, visiting fellow at the Peterson Institute for International Economics, is the Carl J. Shapiro Professor of International Finance at the Brandeis International Business School (IBS) and senior fellow at the East-West Center in Honolulu. He was founding dean of IBS from 1994 to 2006 and has held visiting appointments at the Asian Development Bank Institute, the Brookings Institution, Fudan University, Keio University, Peking University, the Organization for Economic Cooperation and Development, and the World Bank. He also consults for numerous international organizations and governments and serves on the editorial boards of several journals dedicated to Asia-Pacific research. He is the convener of the *East-West Dialogue*, member of the US Asia Pacific Council and the Pacific Trade and Development Conference (PAFTAD) International Steering Committee, and former chair of the US APEC Study Center Consortium. He received AB and PhD degrees in economics from Harvard University.

Michael G. Plummer is the Eni Professor of International Economics at Johns Hopkins University, SAIS Bologna. He is also editor-in-chief of the *Journal of Asian Economics* and (nonresident) senior fellow at the East-West Center. He was head of the Development Division of the Organization for Economic Cooperation and Development (2010–12), associate professor of economics at Brandeis University, and director of its MA programs at the International Business School. He was also a Fulbright Chair in Economics; Pew Fellow in International Affairs, Harvard University; research professor at Kobe University; and visiting fellow at ISEAS, the University of Auckland, and Doshisha University. Plummer has worked on numerous projects for international organizations, development and other government agencies, and regional development banks, including the Asian Development Bank (ADB), the Association for Southeast Nations (ASEAN) Secretariat, and the ADB Institute. He is on the editorial boards of *World Development*, *ASEAN Economic Bulletin*, and *Asian Economic Journal*. He earned his PhD in economics from Michigan State University.

Fan Zhai is managing director and head of the asset allocation and strategy research department of the China Investment Corporation (CIC). He is responsible for overall asset allocation strategy and portfolio management of CIC's overseas investment. He also oversees macroeconomic research and market analysis to support strategic asset allocation and tactical investment views. Before he joined CIC in November 2009, he was research fellow at the Asian Development Bank Institute in Tokyo and economist in the Economics and Research Department of the Asian Development Bank in Manila. He has also worked at the Ministry of Finance and the Development Research Center of the State Council in China. He holds a PhD in system engineering from Huazhong University of Science and Technology, China.

PETER G. PETERSON INSTITUTE FOR INTERNATIONAL ECONOMICS
1750 Massachusetts Avenue, NW
Washington, DC 20036-1903
(202) 328-9000   FAX: (202) 659-3225
www.piie.com

C. Fred Bergsten, *Director*
Edward A. Tureen, *Director of Publications, Marketing, and Web Development*

Copyediting: *Madona Devasahayam*
Typesetting: *BMWW*
Graphics: *Susann Luetjen*
Printing: *United Book Press, Inc.*

Printed in the United States of America
14   13   12   5   4   3   2   1

Library of Congress Cataloging-in-Publication Data
The Trans-Pacific Partnership and Asia-Pacific integration : a quantitative assessment / by Peter A. Petri, Michael G. Plummer, and Fan Zhai.
    p. cm.
Includes bibliographical references and index.
ISBN 978-0-88132-664-2
    1. Trans-Pacific Strategic Economic Partnership Agreement (2005)   2. Asia—Economic integration.   3. Pacific Area—Economic integration.   4. Free trade—Asia.   5. Free trade—Pacific Area.
I. Petri, Peter A., 1946–   II. Plummer, Michael G., 1959–   III. Zhai, Fan.
    HC412.T725 2012
    337.1'1823—dc23

                                    2012037535

Contents

Preface

Engagement with the Asia-Pacific region is crucial for both US economic and foreign policy reasons, and the Trans-Pacific Partnership (TPP)—the 11-country trade agreement now at an advanced stage of negotiations—is the most important current step toward that goal. Over the last two decades, global trade negotiations have stalled and intra-Asian trade pacts have proliferated. Against this background, the TPP would open markets spanning the Pacific and begin to consolidate the "noodle bowl" of nearly 50 existing agreements. It seeks agreement on rules that will be essential for the economy of the 21st century in areas such as services, investment, and intellectual property.

This study provides the first comprehensive quantitative analysis of the potential impact of the TPP on the region and the US economy. It examines these effects in the context of other regional agreements, including those now being negotiated among Asian economies and those already in place. Since the details of these agreements cannot be predicted with certainty, the study focuses on alternative scenarios—based on templates used in the past—and combinations of participants. It provides a roadmap for understanding the potential evolution of the Asia-Pacific trading system and the choices ahead for the United States and other countries in the region. In particular, it posits a two-track evolution of trading arrangements comprising an "Asian track" of Asia-only agreements and a parallel "Pacific track" centered on the TPP, with considerable overlap but also significant differences in membership.

The authors find, most importantly, that the benefits from the TPP and other agreements that would knit this dynamic region together are likely to be substantial. They estimate that world income would rise by $295 billion per year on the TPP track, including by $78 billion per year for the United States.

They also show the benefits from the Asian track and from an eventual merger of the two tracks in a Pacific-wide trade agreement, such as the Free Trade Area of the Asia Pacific (FTAAP) proposed in the Asia-Pacific Economic Cooperation (APEC) forum. They estimate the benefits from such large-scale economic integration at around $2 trillion per year—well in excess of what has been estimated for a successful Doha Round in the World Trade Organization.

The study also shows the importance of achieving a high-quality template in the TPP and subsequent regional trade agreements. In describing the objectives for the TPP, United States Trade Representative Ron Kirk envisions a "high standard, 21st century agreement with a membership and coverage that provides economically significant new market access opportunities for America's workers, farmers, ranchers, service providers, and small businesses." This implies comprehensive coverage; strong rules for services, investment, and intellectual property; and efforts to streamline regulatory impediments to trade. Such an ambitious agreement could ensure that the United States and other advanced economies—which now typically export services and knowledge-intensive products—continue to have a large stake in the expansion of world trade. Wide support for freer trade, in turn, would enable the exports of emerging-market economies to flourish. Thus the benefits of the TPP negotiations are likely to be amplified by a rigorous template, and a subsequent, regionwide agreement based on the TPP could generate much greater benefits than arrangements based on the less ambitious templates typically used in Asian agreements.

The authors examine possible future paths for the TPP and Asian negotiations as they might expand in the years ahead. They argue that the TPP and Asian tracks are likely to compete with each other at first and, in time, many Asia-Pacific economies could become members of both. China and the United States could be among the relatively few countries left *without* preferential access to each other's markets, giving them strong incentive to consolidate the tracks. In this positive scenario, the Trans-Pacific and Asian integration tracks could well lead to comprehensive Asia-Pacific free trade. The study thus provides a powerful example of how "competitive trade liberalization," a strategy initiated and developed in Peterson Institute publications dating from the mid-1990s, could drive market opening despite the challenges now faced by global negotiations.

This study also makes important contributions from a methodological viewpoint. It builds on a long analytical tradition but introduces modeling advances that recognize the importance of the "extensive margin," that is, trade in new products that is made possible by liberalization. The authors also develop a new database to quantify the templates of 47 existing regional and bilateral trade agreements. The study thus incorporates significant advances over prior estimates of the effects of major trade policy changes.

The authors stick closely to economics and objective results in this study, although they recognize that geopolitical dimensions will importantly affect the success of the negotiations. Two of the authors have contributed a separate Policy Brief that pushes beyond the numbers to offer concrete policy recommendations. In that brief, they recommend that the United States and its partners conclude the TPP negotiations quickly and that the negotiators strive to balance high standards in the TPP with the aim of eventually extending the reach of the agreement regionwide. The brief also notes that the TPP may negatively affect some nonparticipating countries, including China, and therefore suggests parallel "bridging" efforts between the TPP and Asian negotiating tracks along with direct cooperation between the United States and China on issues that could impede regionwide free trade in the future.

As beneficial as the TPP can be, its success is not assured. Sensitive issues remain to be addressed by every country, including the United States. The agreement will cover sectors like agriculture, labor, and intellectual property, on which several participants will be reluctant to make concessions. The United States will need to address development concerns of TPP participants with much lower per capita incomes, notably Vietnam. Differences are emerging on many issues, including investment protection, state-owned enterprises, and intellectual property rights. All TPP participants will derive systemic benefits from building a broader Asia-Pacific economic agreement, but countries other than the United States will undertake changes in their sensitive domestic policies only with reciprocal actions by the United States itself.

The Peter G. Peterson Institute for International Economics is a private, nonprofit institution for the study and discussion of international economic policy. Its purpose is to analyze important issues in that area and to develop and communicate practical new approaches for dealing with them. The Institute is completely nonpartisan.

The Institute is funded by a highly diversified group of philanthropic foundations, private corporations, and interested individuals. About 35 percent of the Institute's resources in our latest fiscal year was provided by contributors outside the United States. The Henry Luce Foundation and the United States–Japan Foundation provided generous support for this study.

The Institute's Board of Directors bears overall responsibilities for the Institute and gives general guidance and approval to its research program, including the identification of topics that are likely to become important over the medium run (one to three years) and that should be addressed by the Institute. The director, working closely with the staff and outside Advisory Committee, is responsible for the development of particular projects and makes the final decision to publish an individual study.

The Institute hopes that its studies and other activities will contribute to building a stronger foundation for international economic policy around the world. We invite readers of these publications to let us know how they think we can best accomplish this objective.

C. Fred Bergsten
Director
November 2012

Foreword

The Trans-Pacific and Asian trade negotiations are bright points in an era of sagging economic indicators and international discord. This study is an effort to understand these tracks and their potential impact on individual economies and the global trading system.

Negotiations are a moving target; both tracks are projects in competitive liberalization with shifting membership and strategies. We do not intend, therefore, to offer projections but rather transparent analyses of multiple possibilities. To help readers judge the plausibility of these results, we also provide access to the detailed assumptions and data used to derive them.

Much of the documentation is in this book and more is on the study's website: www.asiapacifictrade.org. The site includes research papers by our team, further detail on published results, the data used in the simulations, additional scenarios that are not presented in this book or are completed after this book goes to press, and links to work by other researchers on related topics. Readers are asked to consult the site for deeper and more recent results and to suggest how the information we develop might be improved to help policymakers and others examine possible outcomes and evaluate simulation methodologies.

We have benefited from much generous advice and support. We are especially grateful to Charles E. Morrison and C. Fred Bergsten, respective heads of the East-West Center and the Peterson Institute for International Economics, and the Brandeis University Asia Pacific Center, the primary sponsors of this work. In addition, we thank John Ballingall, Taeho Bark, Penhong Cai, Kenneth Cukier, Wendy Dobson, Michael Ferrantino, Christopher Findlay, Ellen Frost, Gary Hawke, Gary Horlick, Gary Hufbauer, Stephen Jacobi, Sang-Kyom

Kim, Robert Koopman, Jock Hoi Lim, Warren Maruyama, Andrew McCredie, Rachel McCulloch, Eduardo Pedrosa, Robert Scollay, Jeffrey Schott, Tri Thanh Vo, Barbara Weisel, Jianping Zhang, and Yunling Zhang for comments on drafts and presentations.

We are also grateful for many valuable comments at seminars organized by the Asian Development Bank Institute, the Asia Foundation, the Brunei Darussalam Ministry of Foreign Affairs and Trade, the Central Institute of Economic Management in Vietnam, the Chief Negotiators of the Trans-Pacific Partnership agreement (at the 11th round of negotiations in Melbourne), the China Pacific Economic Cooperation Committee, the East-West Center, the Diplomatic Academy of Vietnam, the Foreign Trade University of Vietnam, the Institute of Developing Economics–JETRO in Tokyo, the Institute for Global Economics in Seoul, the Korea Economic Institute, the Korea Institute of International Economic Policy, the Korean Ministry of Foreign Affairs and Trade, the Malaysian Institute of Strategic and International Studies, the Malaysian Ministry of International Trade and Industry, the University of International Business and Economics in Beijing, the Peterson Institute for International Economics, the Singapore Ministry of Trade, and the United States International Trade Commission.

PETER A. PETRI
MICHAEL G. PLUMMER
FAN ZHAI
November 2012

1

Introduction

Since the conclusion of the Uruguay Round of multilateral trade negotiations in 1994, the development of new international trade rules has shifted from global to bilateral and regional agreements. Bilateral agreements greatly outnumber regional ones, but there is now intense interest in the latter, especially in the Asia-Pacific region. The Trans-Pacific Partnership (TPP), now in negotiation,[1] could become the first significant regional agreement in the Asia-Pacific since the North American Free Trade Agreement (NAFTA) was concluded in 1992. Another "Asian track" of regional initiatives is also in negotiation in Northeast and Southeast Asia. This study provides a quantitative assessment of the benefits and prospects of the two tracks.

The history of large regional initiatives in the Asia-Pacific is not encouraging. An effort to position the Asia-Pacific Economic Cooperation (APEC) forum as a venue for binding agreements ended with the failure of the Early Voluntary Sectoral Liberalization initiative in 1998. Proposals for a Free Trade Area of the Asia-Pacific (FTAAP) were endorsed by APEC leaders in 2009 and 2010 but have gained little traction. Negotiations to create a possible Regional Comprehensive Economic Partnership (RCEP), consisting of 16 Asian and Australasian economies, will likely be launched in November 2012 but will no doubt face many challenges once substantive discussions begin. These initiatives have been hampered by the complexity of the region's history, the sensitivities of diverse partners, and contentious domestic politics.

---

1. The TPP negotiations have 11 official members at this writing: Australia, Brunei Darussalam, Canada, Chile, Malaysia, Mexico, New Zealand, Peru, Singapore, the United States, and Vietnam. Canada and Mexico joined in 2012. Japan has expressed interest, but its participation is still unclear.

The stalemate in global negotiations, however, has increased the urgency of regional efforts. As the center of gravity of world trade shifts toward the Asia-Pacific, this region has an especially large stake in the rules of the international trading system. Against this challenging background, the TPP negotiators are now attempting to fashion a cutting-edge "21st century agreement" (USTR 2011a). The 11 TPP countries account for 36 percent of world trade as an exporter, importer, or both. The negotiations are ambitious in terms of issues and range of members. If successful, they could establish new, high-quality rules for the leading sectors of both emerging-market and advanced economies, keep the "bicycle" of global trade liberalization upright,[2] and yield an innovative model for consolidating existing trade agreements.[3]

An assessment of the Trans-Pacific and Asian tracks of trade agreements has to account for two novel features of the current negotiations. First, both tracks envision enlargements and are therefore essentially multistep games. Indeed, the value of the early negotiations depends more on the template that they establish for future trading relationships than on direct gains. Thus, this study pays close attention to how the tracks might evolve and affect each other. Second, the tracks involve sophisticated, multifaceted economic relationships that span emerging-market and advanced economies. They cover many issues, including so-called new issues such as services, investment, intellectual property, and logistics. We apply new tools of trade theory and assemble new databases to analyze these dimensions in greater depth than was possible in earlier work.

Our results confirm the importance of the TPP and Asian agreements. Of course one cannot account for the full implications of such ambitious initiatives (see box 1.1), but to the extent that they can be measured they appear to be large—indeed, larger than those expected from a successful conclusion of the Doha Development Agenda. Moreover, a comprehensive, high-quality template, such as proposed for the TPP, could roughly double the ultimate gains from regional integration. Strategic interactions between the TPP and Asian tracks also appear to be constructive: Progress on each track is likely to generate incentives for enlargement and for progress on the other track. While the economies effectively driving the tracks—China and the United States—will compete in the early stages, they will face increasing incentives over time to consolidate the tracks into a regionwide agreement. Taken individually and together, the tracks constitute a large, dynamic, positive-sum project.

The study is organized as follows. Chapter 2 reviews the origins of the TPP and the objectives of the United States and other economies. Chapter 3 describes the model, data, and the methodology used to evaluate the TPP and

---

2. As argued by C. Fred Bergsten and William R. Cline (1983, 59–98), liberal trade regimes are inherently unstable and require new initiatives to stay open.

3. The full consolidation of existing agreements within the TPP is not likely to be completed in the initial agreement, but importantly TPP negotiators are committed to establishing common rules of origin and full cumulation of inputs originating within the region.

Box 1.1 What benefits are measured?

The immodest goal of major trade agreements is to change the structures of economies and international economic relationships. Such fundamental changes involve gradual, large, and long processes, shaped in part by feedbacks between economics and politics. Thus, any assessment of the consequences of such agreements, especially before their terms are decided, must begin by recognizing the inherent limitations of the exercise.

This study uses what we believe to be the most advanced analytical framework and empirical information available at this time, but much work remains on both the modeling and data fronts. As the text explains, our model incorporates features that should mitigate problems associated with prior approaches, but it has not yet been tested in ex post evaluations. The model also uses extensive new information but cannot resolve uncertainties about what provisions negotiators will build into future agreements. These uncertainties are reflected in the results: Numerous options are presented, and sensitivity analysis suggests that changes in key assumptions could easily make estimated benefits one-third smaller or larger.

Economic integration may have large additional benefits that are not adequately captured by microeconomic models. Angus Maddison's (2001) path-breaking historical studies show that globalization played a central role in waves of world economic growth in the past. Technology may be the ultimate root of economic progress, but integrated markets dramatically enhance its utilization and pace of development. Maddison finds that rapid globalization helps to explain the acceleration of world economic growth in 1870–1913 and again since World War II, both periods of substantial trade and investment liberalization. He and others also attribute much of the blame for the disastrous results of the interwar period to the collapse of the international economic order. If the trade agreements analyzed in this study can help to sustain rapid globalization, their benefits could be far greater than our computations suggest.

An important limitation—or perhaps strength—of this study is that it focuses on economic results and not domestic or international politics. It does so to keep the results transparent and evidence-based. But there is little doubt that political factors will shape trade policy and economic results will affect politics. These two-way interactions could lead to deeper Asia-Pacific integration and political cooperation at best or to new barriers and political conflict at worst. We argue that the TPP and Asian tracks represent a strongly positive-sum game and will reward the "right" political choices. But we recognize that this alone will not ensure support for the tracks or political will to direct them toward consolidation.

Asian tracks. Chapter 4 analyzes the emerging "contest of templates" between the two tracks. Chapter 5 applies a dynamic, strategic perspective to explore how the tracks are likely to evolve. Chapter 6 presents the results from national viewpoints, analyzing how countries might position themselves in the negotiations, and chapter 7 concludes.

How and Why the Trans-Pacific Partnership Became a Priority

The TPP negotiations are emerging amidst great uncertainty about the global trading system. After more than a decade of work, the Doha Development Agenda has reached an impasse and its future is unclear. Many deadlines have been missed; most recently in December 2011 negotiators were unable to agree even on "alternative deliverables" in lieu of concluding the round. Meanwhile, a powerful wave of bilateral and regional trade agreements has swept across the Asia-Pacific (figure 2.1 and table 2.1). Before 2000, four major agreements had been signed by multiple APEC economies: the ASEAN Free Trade Area,[1] the Canada-US Free Trade Agreement, the North American Free Trade Agreement, and the Australia–New Zealand Closer Economic Relations agreement. By June 2012, 47 agreements had been signed and still others were in negotiation. Many of these agreements link ASEAN countries and Asian and Australasian partners, but the most rapidly expanding subset involves Trans-Pacific relationships.

Historical Roots

The shift from global to bilateral and regional negotiations is rooted in deep political-economic causes: The world economy is becoming multipolar, international linkages are growing more complex, and past agreements have eliminated many of the most tractable trade barriers. Further liberalization

---

1. The ASEAN Free Trade Area is a trade agreement among the ten member countries of the Association of Southeast Asian Nations: Brunei Darussalam, Cambodia, Indonesia, Lao PDR, Malaysia, Myanmar, the Philippines, Singapore, Thailand, and Vietnam.

Figure 2.1   Trends in Asia-Pacific trade agreements, 1982–2012

number of agreements in force

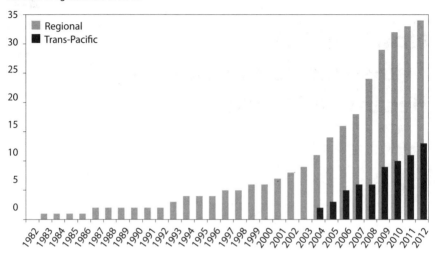

Note: The figure counts only agreements among APEC members. Regional agreements comprise members from only the Americas or only Asia; Trans-Pacific agreements comprise members from the Americas and Asia.

Source: Table 2.1.

now appears to require incremental steps among close partners or on narrow issues. This enables negotiators to focus on important and manageable problems to reduce adjustment costs and mitigate political opposition. However, inconsistencies among many smaller agreements could ultimately limit, rather than encourage, deeper integration. There is no clear framework to guide Asia-Pacific or other regional initiatives in coherent directions. While APEC is committed to achieving "free and open trade and investment in the Asia Pacific," it is not a negotiating forum and cannot do much more than advocate for convergence.

In 2006 four small APEC economies—Brunei Darussalam, Chile, New Zealand, and Singapore—took the bull by the horns and concluded the Trans-Pacific Strategic Economic Partnership (also known as P4) to create a model for a high-quality, regionwide free trade agreement (FTA) (Fergusson and Vaughn 2009, WTO 2008). From early on, P4 members saw their agreement not as an end in itself but as the seed of a broad, Trans-Pacific effort (Elms 2009).

At the close of the George W. Bush administration in September 2008, US Trade Representative Susan Schwab announced US interest in joining the TPP. A year after taking office, President Barack Obama took up the initiative and notified Congress of his intention to create a "high-standard, broad-based regional pact." Other new partners included Australia, Peru, and Vietnam; Malaysia joined in 2010 and Canada and Mexico joined in 2012. At the No-

Table 2.1 Asia-Pacific trade agreements

Agreement	Type	Trade, 2009 (billions of dollars)	Signed	Implemented
Australia–New Zealand	Asia	15.7	1983	1983
Mexico-Peru I	Americas	1.6	1987	1987
AFTA I	Asia	171.7	1992	1993
NAFTA	Americas	951.6	1992	1994
Canada-Chile	Americas	1.9	1996	1997
Chile-Mexico	Americas	4.2	1998	1999
New Zealand–Singapore	Asia	1.2	2000	2001
Japan-Singapore	Asia	24.0	2002	2002
Australia-Singapore	Asia	7.8	2003	2003
Chile-US	Americas	21.0	2003	2004
Singapore-US	Trans-Pacific	54.8	2003	2004
Chile-Korea	Trans-Pacific	5.9	2003	2004
China–Hong Kong	Asia	85.4	2003	2004
ASEAN-China	Asia	455.0	2004	2005
Australia-US	Trans-Pacific	53.1	2004	2005
Australia-Thailand	Asia	13.5	2004	2005
New Zealand–Thailand	Asia	1.6	2005	2005
Japan-Malaysia	Asia	35.2	2005	2006
Korea-Singapore	Asia	15.6	2005	2006
P4	Trans-Pacific	2.5	2005	2006
Chile-China	Trans-Pacific	25.1	2005	2006
Japan-Thailand	Asia	58.3	2007	2007
Chile-Japan	Trans-Pacific	11.7	2007	2007
ASEAN-Korea	Asia	245.1	2006	2007
ASEAN-Japan	Asia	377.1	2008	2008
China–New Zealand	Asia	8.7	2008	2008
Brunei-Japan	Asia	0.8	2007	2008
Indonesia-Japan	Asia	41.1	2007	2008
AFTA II	Asia	171.7	2007	2008
Japan-Philippines	Asia	26.5	2006	2008
Peru-US	Americas	13.8	2006	2009
Japan-Mexico	Trans-Pacific	16.7	2009	2009
Chile-Peru	Americas	2.8	2006	2009

(continued on next page)

Table 2.1   Asia-Pacific trade agreements *(continued)*

Agreement	Type	Trade, 2009 (billions of dollars)	Signed	Implemented
Australia-Chile	Trans-Pacific	0.7	2008	2009
Canada-Peru	Americas	2.7	2008	2009
China-Singapore	Asia	1.5	2008	2009
Japan-Vietnam	Asia	18.1	2008	2009
Singapore-Peru	Trans-Pacific	0.2	2008	2009
ASEAN-Australia-New Zealand	Asia	240.3	2009	2010
Malaysia–New Zealand	Asia	1.4	2009	2010
China-Taiwan	Asia	160.9	2010	2010
China-Peru	Trans-Pacific	9.3	2009	2010
Hong Kong–New Zealand	Asia	1.2	2010	2011
Chile-Malaysia	Trans-Pacific	0.3	2010	2011
Korea-US	Trans-Pacific	101.9	2011	2012
Mexico-Peru II	Americas	1.6	2011	2012
Chile-Vietnam	Trans-Pacific	0.3	2011	2012

Source: Authors' compilation.

vember 2011 APEC Summit negotiators announced the outlines of the TPP agreement (USTR 2011b), and Canada, Japan, and Mexico expressed interest in joining the negotiations. Canada and Mexico have since been invited to participate, but at this writing Japan's participation remains uncertain. Thirteen rounds of intensive negotiations—reportedly including around 400 negotiators in each session—have been completed since March 2010.

Objectives of the TPP

The participation of the United States has added considerable momentum to the TPP while also elevating US concerns among negotiating priorities. Some observers suspect that the United States is promoting the TPP for purely geopolitical reasons, an issue addressed in more detail below. Although geopolitical considerations of course matter, the reasons usually given for US membership—by two different administrations over a five-year period—are straightforward and well justified by economic interests.

Develop 21st century rules. The TPP aims to establish a comprehensive, modern template for economic partnerships. This means tackling more areas than are covered by WTO negotiations (such as environment and labor) and addressing issues related to new economic activities and patterns of linkages, including rules that affect the leading sectors of advanced economies.

Level the playing field. Asian FTAs typically exclude the United States and could divert trade and investment from it; for example, seven of the ten current TPP partners already have FTAs with China, and the possibility of an FTA with China is in negotiation or under discussion with all others. Most also have FTAs with Japan and Korea. The TPP would provide comparable advantages for US producers.

Strengthen linkages with the Asia-Pacific. One-third of world trade—the most rapidly expanding third—is among APEC economies. Asia-Pacific economic relationships complement broad US foreign policy interests: "America's future is linked to the future of the Asia-Pacific region; and the future of this region depends on America."[2]

Consolidate existing trade agreements. Trade among pairs or groups of APEC countries is now covered by 47 bilateral or regional trade agreements, and of these 23 offer preferences to trade among the 11 countries expected to participate in the TPP negotiations (see table 2.1). Inconsistent provisions and/or rules of origin are burdensome for firms with multicountry operations. The United States intends to avoid negotiating further bilateral FTAs and seeks to consolidate the "noodle bowl" of current Asia-Pacific trade rules.

Additional reasons sometimes mentioned are that the TPP could support President Obama's targets to double exports by 2014 and to create jobs for the US economic recovery. This study examines only the microeconomic effects of the TPP agreement—on trade, incomes, and employment—and finds that those variables are unlikely to be affected significantly before 2015. To be sure, an early, path-breaking agreement could stimulate economic activity through investor expectations, if markets interpret economic integration through the TPP as a positive predictor of growth in the United States and the Asia-Pacific region. Such effects are difficult to assess and are not examined in this study.

We have not attempted to catalogue the reasons for participation by other countries,[3] but our results suggest that potential economic gains are significant for most countries, especially for smaller developing economies with large initial barriers. Moreover, many countries will benefit from joining both tracks, thus gaining preferential access to both Chinese and American markets, among others. These benefits may be reinforced by political advantages; trade agreements can support domestic reforms and secure more balanced relationships with regional superpowers.

---

2. US Secretary of State Hillary Clinton, remarks on Regional Architecture in Asia: Principles and Priorities, Imin Center-Jefferson Hall, Honolulu, Hawaii, January 12, 2010, www.state.gov/secretary/rm/2010/01/135090.htm (accessed on September 11, 2012).

3. See Aggarwal and Lee (2011) and Ravenhill (2009) for political perspectives in several countries.

Geopolitics

Despite a compelling list of economic priorities, some observers argue that the TPP has a purely geopolitical agenda, namely containing China. For example, one prominent Australian scholar believes that "America's vision is that Asia will divide into two camps, with China on one side and the rest, under US leadership, on the other ... thus restoring America's uncontested primacy" and that the TPP is merely the "economic element" of this plan.[4] Others call the TPP a "geopolitical and diplomatic power play, and a kind of economic warfare within the Asia Pacific region."[5] Meanwhile, a respected American scholar sees Asian integration as an effort to achieve Chinese hegemony at the expense of the United States, ominously noting that the Peloponnesian War in 431 BC was caused by "the growth of Athenian power and the fear which this caused in Sparta" (Friedberg 2011). Unfortunately, such overwrought narratives take on a life of their own and lend credibility to each other. They see trade policy in zero-sum terms and therefore argue that it must serve hidden, hegemonic objectives. By distorting the public debate, they make it difficult to find pragmatic solutions to real concerns.

Of course, there is strategic competition between China and the United States, and it cannot be fully separated from the TPP and Asian trade negotiations. The decision by the United States to sustain its security role in Asia boosted the Obama administration's interest in the economic relationships offered by the TPP. Also, China's interest in "strategic space" in Asia is no doubt a reason for the trade and financial agreements and other economic initiatives that China is pursuing with Northeast Asian and ASEAN neighbors. Paradoxically, this competition may lead to more open policies and greater interdependence also between China and the United States. In this strategic context, even if the TPP and Asian tracks make good economic sense, they could exacerbate "strategic distrust" in the China-US relationship (Lieberthal and Wang 2012).

One way to minimize such tensions would be to avoid smaller agreements altogether and embark on a new global or regionwide negotiation that includes China and the United States. But even aside from the sheer complexity of this effort—rivaling the Doha Round in its difficulty—this strategy does not appear to be feasible for now. One major obstacle is macroeconomics: In China and especially in the United States, such vast negotiations would raise wide opposition in a weak global economy. Given uncertain prospects, China and the United States would be likely to raise, and unlikely to agree on, many controversial issues ranging from state-owned enterprises, trade remedies, and services liberalization to technology exports, the protection of intellectual

---

4. Hugh White, "Dear Mr. President, We Beg to Differ over the Future of Asia," *Sydney Morning Herald,* November 16, 2011, www.smh.com.au/opinion/politics/dear-mr-president-we-beg-to-differ-over-the-future-of-asia-20111115-1nh36.html (accessed on September 11, 2012).

5. Anthony Rowley, "What the TPP Is Really About," *Business Times (Singapore),* February 2, 2011.

property, and labor freedoms. Moreover, domestic interests in each country could also force insoluble social, financial, and security issues onto the agenda.

A feasible alternative is to pursue parallel liberalization tracks for now but to manage the competition between them so that a foundation emerges for convergence. The two tracks are bound to continue in parallel until the differences between their provisions narrow and more favorable economic and political conditions develop for bridging them. But conditions can improve over time as interdependence deepens, especially if active efforts are made to promote cooperation and trust along the way. The tracks should help: They will reduce obstacles to integration—including adjustment costs—and, over time, amplify the gains to China and the United States from consolidated trade rules.

This strategy also argues for direct cooperation between China and the United States alongside the TPP and Asian negotiations. Both countries must recognize and address the suspicions generated by the TPP and Asian tracks. A separate paper by two of us proposes policy strategies for doing so (Petri and Plummer 2012). It suggests reducing substantive differences between the TPP and Asian tracks and pursuing a "third track" of discussions between China and the United States—built on the Strategic and Economic Dialogue—to minimize misunderstandings and to pave the way for the consolidation of the tracks. This third track could gradually and systematically tackle policy differences between the two countries that stand in the way of a regionwide agreement. Competition is part of any intense economic relationship and does not imply apocalyptic outcomes. Properly managed, the TPP and Asian tracks could become the seeds for regional and possibly global cooperation on an unprecedented scale.

Competing Templates

From the viewpoint of large economies like China and the United States, early and relatively small regional trade agreements provide a way to influence the future of the regional and perhaps global trading systems. The much-remarked competition between the Trans-Pacific and Asian tracks is thus really a "contest of templates" for organizing future cooperation, not economic warfare, between them. From an economic perspective, no country can benefit from dividing the region into blocs, but countries could gain from entrenching rules that improve the terms of integration for their strongest sectors.

If the core strategy of the TPP is to develop comprehensive, high-quality rules, then the Asian track seeks most importantly to strengthen the production chains that connect many countries in the region. Asian agreements also prioritize inclusiveness—ASEAN agreements, for example, often mention reducing intraregional disparities as an objective—and are more willing to include exceptions for products that are sensitive to countries or interest groups. These broad differences translate into many specific contrasts. High-quality trade agreements involve sophisticated disciplines that constrict policy space; inclusive rules aim for a common denominator accessible to diverse economies.

These contrasts can be documented based on comparisons of recent Asian and US agreements. To gain insight into the structure of different agreements and to provide a rigorous basis for simulating their effects, we collected detailed information on the provisions of the 47 bilateral and regional agreements concluded by APEC economies (those listed in table 2.1) as they addressed 21 major issues that frequently appear in such agreements. This analysis, described more fully in appendix C and based in part on information developed by APEC and the WTO, offers a novel quantitative window on the content of trade agreements.

Both recent US and ASEAN trade agreements have included large eventual reductions in tariffs (96 and 90 percent of most favored nation [MFN] levels, respectively), but US agreements have been quicker to take effect and have had fewer exceptions than ASEAN agreements. Since ASEAN tariffs are also higher initially, the net effect is to leave more barriers behind.

The templates differ even more in provisions that address nontariff barriers. To assess these differences, we constructed "scores" for how each agreement addressed 21 issues, using a classification that bridges those used by APEC and the WTO in organizing the underlying data. The scores are designed to be as objective as possible and are derived from quantifiable dimensions of the text of the underlying agreements. They account for three dimensions of the provisions addressing each issue: (1) the proportion of potential disciplines on an issue that were covered, (2) the depth of such coverage, and (3) the enforceability of provisions. Each agreement on each issue has a score between 0 and 1; 0 means that the agreement did not address the issue at all, and 1 means that the agreement was among the top 10 percent of agreements that had the most rigorous provisions on the issue. Most scores fall in between, depending on actual coverage.

Figure 2.2 compares agreements concluded by the United States and ASEAN since 2006. US agreements had higher scores than ASEAN agreements on average, perhaps because more rigorous provisions are possible and expected in the more extensive legal environment of the United States. But ASEAN agreements also had higher scores in a few areas, including dispute resolution and cooperation (typically provisions on capacity building). The contrast between the templates is most evident in scores that are substantially different. This is the case for issues such as competition, intellectual property rights, government procurement, state-owned enterprises, and labor. Neither set of agreements had high marks on small and medium enterprises and science and technology, areas that are also expected to be covered by the TPP.

What explains these differences? Asian templates are negotiated by mainly emerging-market economies with comparative advantages in manufacturing—hence the focus on market access for goods. The templates negotiated by the United States reflect the interests of advanced economies in services, investment, intellectual property, and sometimes agriculture. They also emphasize rules-based approaches that are common in a developed-country institutional setting. Both templates include measures to attract domestic

Figure 2.2   Average scores of provisions in recent Asia-Pacific FTAs

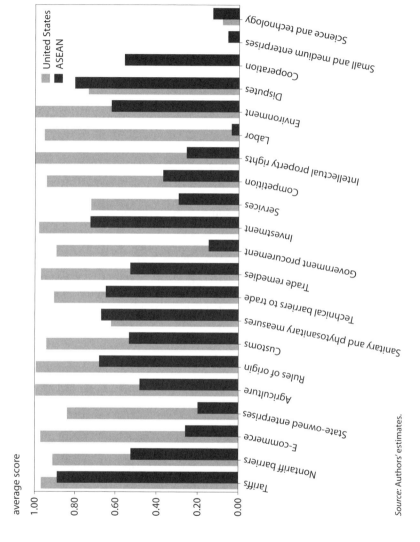

average score

Source: Authors' estimates.

political support, but those too differ because of their political setting: Asian agreements focus on cooperation and technology, and US agreements on labor and the environment.

Since potential gains from trade are especially significant among diverse economies, the ideal template will offer market access for the manufacturing industries of emerging-market countries as well as good rules for the services, investment, and technology sectors of advanced countries.[6] This is increasingly important in a setting where production systems are fragmented and span several types of activities and many countries; activities classified as services are often critical inputs in manufacturing, and vice versa. While Asian templates prepare the ground for greater cooperation by addressing primarily goods liberalization, US templates attempt to liberalize sectors that lead in both types of economies, ideally expanding opportunities for trade and production linkages between them.

The Emerging TPP Template

The details of the prospective TPP agreement remain uncertain, but the likely structure of the agreement is summarized in table 2.2. This table is based on the outline released by negotiators in November 2011, which comprised 20 specific issues and 4 cross-cutting issues (listed in the table as items 21 to 24). The issues overlap substantially with the categories of our analysis of past agreements. If this structure persists, most TPP provisions will deal with "behind the border" issues, addressing deep economic linkages that require coherent national regulations. These provisions are bound to generate disagreements among TPP partners and potential future members since they address policies that have been traditionally managed domestically. Some controversies that are already emerging are highlighted in table 2.2.

The TPP negotiations not only span diverse issues and economies but also cover ground already subject to many FTAs. Negotiators are attempting to address this complexity by highlighting cross-cutting issues such as regulatory coherence, competitiveness and business facilitation, promotion of small and medium enterprises, and deeper production and supply chain linkages. With respect to obligations under prior FTAs, a messy, hybrid approach appears to have emerged, leaving it up to countries to decide whether to keep old FTAs or rewrite them and whether to make new offers on a bilateral or multilateral basis (Barfield 2011). But the most vexing problem of the "noodle bowl"—the restrictive effect of inconsistent rules of origin—is likely to be solved; negotiators are committed to establishing common rules of origin that permit the cumulation of inputs across all member economies.

---

6. Gary Clyde Hufbauer, Jeffrey Schott, and Woan Foong Wong (2010) argue that the lack of such symmetry helps to explain why the Doha Development Agenda received little support in advanced economies.

Table 2.2 The Trans-Pacific Partnership as a 21st century agreement

Issue	Mostly behind border?	Content	Controversies
1 Competition	Yes	Traditionally a limited chapter that requires parties to maintain competition laws and to ensure that designated monopolies do not impede competition. The United States has proposed substantially expanded disciplines to ensure "competitive neutrality" in the treatment of state-owned enterprises, including provisions on transparency, consumer protection, and private rights of action.	Under US proposals economies that have a significant state-owned sector could face significant reform requirements. Disclosure and enforcement requirements are controversial.
2 Cooperation and capacity building	Yes	Enhance ability of developing-country members to participate in negotiations and implement the agreement; create demand-driven and flexible institutional mechanisms to facilitate cooperation and capacity building.	Uncontroversial in principle but extent of support remains to be negotiated.
3 Cross-border services	Yes	Secure fair, open, and transparent markets for services; require national and most favored nation (MFN) treatment; bar performance requirements; require regulations to be transparent and not unduly burdensome; ensure transfers and payments; address licenses and certifications obtained abroad; negotiate comprehensive market access subject only to exceptions on a "negative list" of nonconforming measures.	Controversial; the diversity of services and limited prior multilateral liberalization make the negotiations difficult. Advanced economies seek broad and strict disciplines; emerging-market economies seek exclusions and slow implementation. Since all Trans-Pacific Partnership (TPP) members have traditionally excluded some sectors from past free trade agreements, this is likely to be a difficult negotiation.
4 Customs	No	Establish customs procedures that are predictable, transparent, and fast, with explicit goal of supporting regional production networks and supply chains.	High priority for most economies but emerging-market economies are concerned about implementation costs and schedules; technical assistance may be helpful (see "Cooperation and capacity building").

(continued on next page)

Table 2.2 The Trans-Pacific Partnership as a 21st century agreement *(continued)*

Issue	Mostly behind border?	Content	Controversies
5 E-commerce	Yes	Ensure free flow of information across borders; prohibit tariffs on e-commerce; facilitate cross-border supply of services and authentication of e-transactions; protect confidentiality of information. May include additional accords on information flows and treatment of digital products.	Issues involving the regulation of information flow are of concern to some economies.
6 Environment	Yes	Require laws for environmental protection and effective remedies for violations; require adherence to multilateral agreements such as the Convention on International Trade in Endangered Species of Wild Fauna and Flora (CITES) and the Montreal Protocol; ensure public participation; encourage technological cooperation; authorize joint committees; proposals on new issues, such as conservation, biodiversity, invasive alien species, climate change, and environmental goods and services.	Some economies seek higher environmental standards than others; developing economies want safeguards against "environmental protectionism."
7 Financial services	Yes	Ensure protection of investments, nondiscrimination, and transparency of regulation; limit caps on institutions and transactions; establish consultations and dispute resolution including investor-state arbitration; possibly specific disciplines for postal entities.	Controversial, particularly in light of global financial crises; some advanced countries seek comprehensive services sector access.
8 Government procurement	Yes	Require transparency, national treatment, and nondiscrimination consistent with the World Trade Organization's (WTO) Government Procurement Agreement (GPA); specify rules of origin; establish standards for transparency; provide for supplier challenges; allow for transitional measures in developing economies. Requires negotiation of list of covered entities.	Only two TPP economies have acceded to WTO accords; three others are observers. Members will push for strong provisions and observers will likely follow, but nonmembers will seek high de minimis rules. Transitional measures could be controversial.

9	Intellectual property rights	Yes	Require accession to international treaties; require effective enforcement of criminal and civil penalties in case of know-ing violations; require destruction of pirated or counterfeit goods; proposals on trademarks, geographical indications, copyrights, patents, trade secrets, data for the approval of genetic resources and traditional knowledge. Proposed pro-visions go well beyond the WTO Agreement on Trade Related Aspects of Intellectual Property Rights (TRIPS) on copyright, patent, and data exclusivity terms and on enforcement.	Highly controversial, involves pharmaceuticals, copyright-based industries, and online services. Exporters seek provisions beyond the TRIPS agreement, such as accession to World Intellectual Property Organization (WIPO) treaties. Stricter provisions face strong opposition from importers, competitive producers, national health systems, online ser-vice providers, and nongovernmental organizations (NGOs).
10	Investment	Yes	Require national and MFN treatment and adherence to minimum standards of treatment under international law; bar performance requirements; require reasonable compensation in case of expropriation; ensure free and timely transfers; establish procedures for investor-state arbitration by international tribunals.	High priority for all TPP economies and multinational companies, but differences exist on sectoral coverage and ownership limits. Investor-state arbitration provisions are strongly opposed by NGOs and some governments, espe-cially as they might affect public health and capital account regulations.
11	Labor	Yes	Incorporate the International Labor Organization (ILO) Declaration; adopt mechanisms to ensure cooperation, coordination, and dialogue on issues of mutual concern; require domestic laws to be consistent with international standards; may require enforcement; authorize joint oversight committees.	Controversial; some developed countries seek labor prac-tices that may be difficult to adopt and may impede com-petitiveness in low-income countries; enforcement could be seen as a sovereignty issue.
12	Legal issues	No	Define rules for administration of the agreement; address issues related to government-to-government dispute settlement and create procedures for convening panels; authorize monetary penalties and suspension of benefits when dispute resolution fails; permit some exceptions from obligations and transparency requirements.	Relatively uncontroversial but may be complicated to recon-cile with national legal requirements.
13	Market access for goods	No	Provide for ambitious, balanced, and transparent improvements in market access; eliminate tariff and nontariff barriers; specify customs valuation methodology; establish oversight committees; provide for exceptions and special treatment of sensitive products. May offer provisions on agricultural export competition and food security.	Difficult negotiations lie ahead on exclusion lists and time path of liberalization; advanced countries may resist reduc-ing barriers on labor-intensive goods. Some agricultural products, including sugar and dairy, involve strong offensive and defensive interests.

(continued on next page)

Table 2.2   The Trans-Pacific Partnership as a 21st century agreement *(continued)*

Issue	Mostly behind border?	Content	Controversies
14 Rules of origin	No	Establish rules for determining when a product originates in the free trade agreement; set de minimis standards; establish cumulation rules; list exceptions; provide for verification, documentation, and consultation.	Negotiations involve product-by-product detail. Liberal rules are supported by most countries, but there is strong special-interest opposition to such rules in textiles, footwear and autos—critical industries for some exporting countries. Establishing common rules with cumulation will be an important test of the TPP's ability to consolidate the "noodle bowl."
15 Sanitary and phytosanitary standards (SPS)	Yes	Ensure protection of human, animal, and plant health; reinforce and build on existing rights and obligations under the WTO; include new commitments on science, transparency, regionalization, cooperation, and equivalence; adopt bilateral and multilateral cooperative proposals on import checks and verification.	Will need to address complicated details. Less advanced economies will seek de minimis rules, assurances against hidden protectionism, and technical assistance. An important issue is whether national SPS standards will be subject to international dispute settlement.
16 Technical barriers to trade (TBT)	Yes	Build on WTO Agreement on Technical Barriers to Trade to facilitate trade and protect health, safety, and the environment; commit to compliance periods, conformity assessment.	Advanced economies seek WTO+ features. Developing economies want to avoid ambitious TBT measures and may require technical assistance to implement new provisions.
17 Telecommunications	Yes	Ensure interconnection and nondiscriminatory access to telecommunication networks; eliminate investment limits; assure technology neutrality; promote mutual recognition in testing and certification; require transparency in regulatory and rights of appeal processes.	Principles uncontroversial, but some economies will want to maintain limitations on investment and competition and the development of standards.
18 Temporary entry	No	Provide for short-term entry of businesspersons on an expedited basis; enhance technical cooperation between TPP authorities; prescribe obligations on specific categories of businessperson.	Issues arise on qualifications of service providers; developing countries wish to facilitate liberal access; politically controversial in some developed economies.

19	Textiles and apparel	No	Provide additional rules beyond those required under market access for goods relating to customs cooperation, enforcement procedures, rules of origin, and possibly special safeguards.	This is a critical sector for developing economies and is controversial in light of high unemployment in developed economies. The most difficult negotiations focus on defining rules of origin.
20	Trade remedies	No	Build on WTO rights and obligations in the areas of transparency and due process; include proposals on transitional regional safeguards; limit the scale and duration of safeguard actions.	While the application of trade remedies is often controversial, the proposals do not now call for international review, as provided, for example, by chapter 19 of the North American Free Trade Agreement (NAFTA).
21	Regulatory coherence	Yes	Require regulations to be developed in an open, transparent process; require national treatment, cost-benefit analysis, and centralized review for agreed sectors.	Objectives are relatively uncontroversial, but implementation has little precedent. Some economies prefer a nonbinding approach.
22	Competitiveness and business facilitation	Yes	Provide for cooperation in trade and investment promotion, customs clearance, inspections, and quarantine; create joint working groups.	Relatively uncontroversial; opportunity to support capacity building in low-income economies.
23	Small and medium enterprises (SMEs)	Yes	Promote joint strategies to support SMEs; facilitate capacity building and the dissemination of information.	Relatively uncontroversial; opportunity to support capacity building in low-income economies.
24	Development	Yes	Support development by promoting market liberalization, effective institutions and governance mechanisms; assist countries in implementing the agreement to fully realize benefits.	Uncontroversial in principle but extent of support remains to be negotiated.

Source: Authors' judgments using USTR (2011b) as a starting point. Warren H. Maruyama provided very helpful suggestions.

At least four important fault lines have emerged in the negotiations so far. First, much debate surrounds intellectual property rights (IPRs), with the United States advocating stricter provisions than were included in past agreements, including WTO's Agreement on Trade-Related Aspects of Intellectual Property Rights (TRIPS). Since most TPP economies are net IPR importers, several have challenged the need to go beyond TRIPS. The outcome of this debate will affect the division of benefits between IPR exporters and importers, and perhaps intracountry income distributions. For example, a strict IPR regime could make free entertainment less easily available on the internet, and some types of products, including pharmaceuticals, more expensive in some countries. The issues are complicated by the ubiquitous challenge of protecting IPRs in a dynamic and decentralized online environment.

Second, "competitive neutrality" for state-owned enterprises (SOEs) appears to be emerging as an important and contentious issue. The objective, likely to be addressed through transparency and governance requirements, is to prevent SOEs from gaining competitive advantage from regulatory and tax benefits or through access to capital and other inputs at below-market prices. The proposed rules are not yet public, but observers are concerned that TPP disciplines will be so tough as to preclude future accession by any economy with a large state-owned sector, such as China. In any case, the terms will have to be acceptable to countries like Vietnam and Singapore, which also have large SOE sectors.

Third, provisions for investor-state arbitration of disputes related to foreign investments are generating significant opposition from NGOs and some governments. Such provisions allow corporations to challenge government rulings in tribunals operated by the United Nations and the World Bank and are said to create a "chilling effect" on government regulations (Productivity Commission 2010). In practice, hundreds of bilateral investment treaties (BITs) have included such provisions for 60 years with modest utilization. They are also incorporated into the ASEAN Comprehensive Investment Area, which went into effect in March 2012. A famous recent case involves Australian regulation of cigarette packaging, which has been challenged by tobacco manufacturers as "expropriation without compensation" under the Australia–Hong Kong BIT. Arbitration rulings have upheld regulations motivated for public health purposes in the past, but the TPP negotiators are also said to be considering specific exemptions for tobacco.

Fourth, labor provisions based on the International Labor Organization's (ILO) core labor standards, which include rights of association and collective bargaining, appear to be important for advanced economies, in part reflecting pressures from their own labor unions. The ILO standards are not enforceable, and many TPP countries, including the United States, have not ratified them. Since some political systems currently limit labor organizations—for example, in Vietnam—these provisions complicate the negotiations and may make it harder to consolidate the TPP and Asian tracks in the future.

These disagreements reflect partly differences between more and less advanced economies and partly contrasts in political orientation. At an early stage, the negotiations may also reflect extreme positions by negotiators to satisfy domestic constituents. Eventually, the gaps will have to be bridged, and an agreement should be achievable, given political support at the highest levels of government. Interestingly, the TPP is relatively free so far of one thorny problem that confronts many negotiations: Most parties are net agricultural exporters or have little domestic agriculture.[7] Thus, the general issue of agricultural protection is playing a relatively minor role in the negotiations, except for isolated problems involving sugar and dairy products. However, strict provisions on agriculture could make future enlargements difficult; Canada's entry will provide a test case, but Japanese participation could complicate the negotiations even further.

The fact that several of the new issues prioritized by the TPP concern leading sectors for the United States should not come as a surprise. Advanced economies also led the liberalization of goods trade in earlier global rounds, at a time when they had comparative advantage in them. Those liberalization efforts later facilitated industrialization elsewhere. The new industries in which advanced countries now seek better rules are also likely to open markets for countries and firms that cannot be identified today. The point of a comprehensive template is not that it represents US interests (although that point will be emphasized in the United States by those who favor the TPP, and in other countries by those who oppose it) but that it expands the scope of liberalization and thus potential gains to all participants.

---

7. The United States, Australia, New Zealand, Malaysia, Chile, and Vietnam are net agricultural exporters, and Singapore and Brunei have tiny agricultural sectors and have essentially free trade in agriculture. Canada and Mexico are also net exporters, although Canada has significant import barriers as well. Peru is a net importer of agricultural goods but only marginally so; in 2007 exports were worth $2 billion and imports $2.3 billion (Food and Agriculture Organization, *FAO Statistical Yearbook,* 2009).

3

Analytical Approach

We estimate the effects of Trans-Pacific and Asian integration using an advanced, 18-sector, 24-region, computable general equilibrium (CGE) model of the world economy. Since the agreements we analyze have not yet been concluded, we also have to estimate the potential structure of their provisions. We consider below some of the pitfalls of such an ex ante assessment and the solutions we have adopted to address them.

The Model

The CGE model used in this study, developed by one of us (Zhai 2008), incorporates recent theoretical advances that emphasize firm heterogeneity as a factor in explaining trade flows. In this framework, trade liberalization affects not only sectoral specialization patterns but also the range of goods and services available for consumption and production and the distribution of firms with different productivity levels in the output mix. The model has been previously applied to Asia-Pacific economic integration in studies of the ASEAN Economic Community (Petri, Plummer, and Zhai 2012) and of the long-term development prospects of ASEAN, China, and India (Petri and Zhai 2012). The model provides detailed results on income, trade, production, demand, and employment. Further technical information on the model is provided in appendix A.

Firm heterogeneity appears to be part of the answer to an important puzzle in the empirical analysis of trade liberalization. CGE models have long been the workhorse of trade policy analysis, but recent ex post evaluations have shown that these models have systematically underestimated actual effects. For example, Timothy Kehoe (2005) found that ex ante CGE models of the effects of NAFTA predicted that Mexico's exports would increase by less than 50 percent in most sectors, whereas regional trade relative to GDP actually increased tenfold between 1988 and 1999. Similar results have been also found in European data.

One reason for these errors is that conventional CGE models only track changes in trade by established exporters (the intensive margin of trade). Recent empirical evidence shows, however, that the entry of new exporting firms (the extensive margin of trade) is an especially important consequence of trade liberalization (Hummels and Klenow 2005; Eaton, Kortum, and Kramarz 2004; Kehoe and Ruhl 2003). This finding is confirmed in appropriately structured simulations. Comparing the results generated by a model that incorporates firm heterogeneity with those from a conventional specification, Zhai (2008) found that the heterogeneous model—a smaller version of the model used in this application—predicts more than twice the income gains generated with standard assumptions.

Prior work on Asia-Pacific trade agreements has relied on conventional CGE approaches and is subject to the usual limitations. Moreover, few estimates have explored agreements that include the United States, except in the context of regionwide agreements such as the FTAAP.[1] Even fewer studies have focused on the TPP itself. Some exceptions are Li and Whalley (2012), which examined the effects of the TPP on China; Kawasaki (2010), which focused on Japan; and Itakura and Lee (2012), which was primarily interested in sectoral adjustments under various dynamic scenarios.

Analyzing the TPP and other prospective agreements requires an appropriate model as well as good estimates of the provisions that are likely to be included in an agreement. Most studies use very simple shortcuts to represent future agreements, such as the full elimination of intraregional tariffs and nontariff barriers (when estimated). Such assumptions lead to the overestimation of benefits, since actual agreements involve compromises. The Australian Productivity Commission (2010, xxix) has sharply criticized such efforts, arguing that "the results of modeling in feasibility studies are used to 'oversell' the benefits of agreements, while typically the actual text of agreements is not subject to assessment."[2] To address this bias, the report recommended that studies emphasize multiple scenarios of agreements, transparency of assumptions, and attention to agreement detail.[3]

---

1. These studies include Kawai and Wignaraja (2008), Kawasaki (2010), Park (2006), Park, Park, and Kim (2010), Petri (1997), and Scollay and Gilbert (2000).

2. The United States does conduct a detailed assessment of the texts of proposed agreements through the US International Trade Commission (USITC), such as the assessment of the Korea-US FTA (USITC 2010). The analysis is provided only after an agreement is completed, in preparation for its consideration by Congress.

3. It also recommended that an independent body oversee feasibility studies of future Australian negotiations.

We address these and other potential pitfalls of ex ante analysis in multiple ways. First, we model numerous alternative agreements at considerable levels of detail and conduct sensitivity tests to determine how the results might change with different assumptions (see appendix F). Second, we develop new information on the structure of existing trade agreements in the Asia-Pacific to assess how they address various trade and investment issues and to provide a basis for estimating the content of future agreements. Since we do not have "actual text" for the prospective agreements that we model, we estimate their structure using data from the most relevant existing agreements. Third, we attempt to explain fully all key assumptions and the information on which they are based.

Baseline Projections

Most CGE studies of trade agreements conduct simulations around a single historical data point (typically the latest year available for the Global Trade Analysis Project [GTAP] model, currently 2007). Income and trade effects are then calculated by finding the alternative equilibrium that would have prevailed in the base year, had the agreement been fully implemented along with all structural adjustments. The results are expressed in percentage terms, under the assumption that those would be unaffected by other changes that are likely to occur in the time required to reach and implement an agreement.

Since the Asia-Pacific region is highly dynamic and it might take a decade or more to reach and implement complex agreements, this study adopts a more fine-grained approach. We construct an annual, 15-year baseline path and then simulate agreements by introducing changes in that path. This methodology is more data and computation intensive, but it accounts for expected changes in the relative sizes of economies and the sectoral composition of output, trade, and employment. Year-by-year results also make it possible to examine issues such as the adjustment implications of an agreement.

The baseline path of GDP for the model's 24 countries and regions was calculated by calibrating the model to International Monetary Fund (IMF) projections through 2015 and then to Centre d'Etudes Prospectives et d'Informations Internationales (CEPII) projections until 2025 (Fouré, Bénassy-Quéré, and Fontagné 2010). CEPII uses growth models estimated on the basis of historical labor, capital, and energy time-series data to project future rates of productivity growth, savings, and capital accumulation. The baseline solution also includes the effects of all trade agreements that had been signed by 2010 but were not yet fully implemented in 2007, the year of the model's database (these include most of the agreements listed in table 2.1 in chapter 2).

Baseline projections for output, exports, imports, and outward and inward foreign investment are reported in appendix B. The projections show substantial growth in the world economy: By 2025 GDP will expand by 77 percent, trade will nearly double, and foreign direct investment (FDI) stocks will increase 2.5-fold. The projections also show that the United States, China, and Europe will become roughly similar-sized economies. These large changes affect the importance of different types of agreements and provisions in them. Such long-term projections are of course speculative (at this writing the initial years of the path look too optimistic), but our primary interest is still in *deviations* from the baseline, and they should be relatively insensitive to the details of the growth path.

Scenarios of Trade Agreements

The Trans-Pacific and Asian tracks of negotiations provide a logical way to organize the main simulation scenarios of the study. Each track is assumed to progress through multiple stages of enlargement.[4] Given much uncertainty about the pace of these tracks, the timing assumptions are necessarily arbitrary. Yet the results suggest that the directions are compelling, in the sense that the structure of assumptions made about each track is consistent with the incentives that emerge from the simulations. The two-track approach avoids a flat comparison of many alternatives, focusing instead on major, incentive-consistent trajectories.

Our assumptions about the tracks are summarized in figure 3.1. These scenarios are based on membership assumptions that cannot be predicted accurately. While the general conclusions derived from the results remain intact so far, the likely configuration of the first stage of the TPP has already changed since the present results were calculated. Details of revised scenarios will be published from time to time on our website (www.asiapacifictrade.org). Each track is assumed to progress on an ambitious timeline, in terms of both when agreements are reached and how long it takes to implement them. These timelines represent plausible, but aggressively timed, sequences of policy changes that squeeze implementation and results into a compact time period.

The point of departure for the *Trans-Pacific track* is the P4 agreement, NAFTA, and bilateral agreements connecting several pairs of potential members. Its first new step, assumed to be signed in 2013 and implemented over the 2014–18 period, would be the completion of the nine-country agreement. The next step, assumed to be signed one year later in 2014, would add Canada, Japan, Korea, and Mexico.[5] This enlargement would be implemented over

---

4. Economists concerned with enlargement emphasize making agreements open through automatic accession criteria. In practice, accession usually involves some new negotiations and sometimes even the substitution of a new agreement for an old one. This happened when the Canada-US FTA was expanded into NAFTA and also appears to be happening now with the conversion of the P4 agreement into the TPP.

5. Korea has not expressed official interest in joining the TPP so far. Korea has good access to the US market through the Korea-US FTA, and its immediate priority is to gain similar access to the Chinese markets through a bilateral or trilateral agreement. But senior Korean policymakers have repeatedly signaled their continuing interest in the TPP and Korean membership is probable in the medium term. While the timing of the scenario is thus quite uncertain, its structure is highly probable, and it is the structure that will mainly determine results in, say, 2025.

Figure 3.1 Scenarios for the Trans-Pacific and Asian tracks

Source: Authors' illustration.

2015–19. Thus, the TPP is envisioned to become a 13-member group that includes large, trade-oriented economies across the Pacific.

The point of departure for the *Asian track* is the ASEAN Free Trade Area, the ASEAN Economic Community Blueprint, and numerous bilateral agreements, including between ASEAN and China, Japan, and Korea. Its first new step would be the completion of the China-Japan-Korea agreement, now scheduled to begin negotiations in late 2012. We assume that this agreement will be signed in 2013 and implemented over 2014–18. The second step, assumed to be agreed by 2016 and implemented over 2016–20, would join the China-Japan-Korea and ASEAN agreements into an ASEAN+3 agreement. (Alternatively, Asian integration might proceed through the RCEP agreement that also includes Australia, New Zealand, and India.) While an ASEAN+3 accord may not generate new bilateral liberalization given the existing accords, it should allow regionwide cumulation of rules of origin, and in our modeling approach that yields trade and income gains. The timing assumptions about the Asian track are optimistic (Zhiming 2011), perhaps even more so than the assumptions made about the TPP track.

Importantly, the tracks could continue to a broad, regionwide agreement (on the right-hand side of figure 3.1). We conduct additional simulations to explore the implications of transforming one or both tracks into the FTAAP with membership that includes all economies on the two tracks plus Russia and Taiwan.[6] Since this endpoint could be approached from either track, its

---

6. These two economies are APEC members that are not involved in either TPP or Asian track agreements. It is also convenient to assume that the small "other ASEAN" economies (Cambodia, Lao PDR, and Myanmar) will be ultimately included in the FTAAP, although they are not currently members of APEC.

Figure 3.2   TPP and Asian pathways to the FTAAP

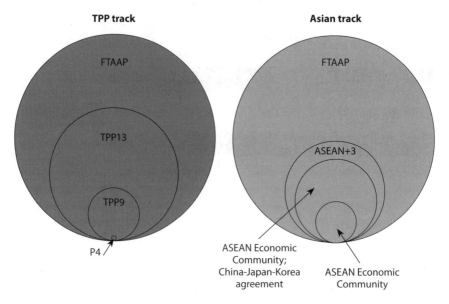

Note: Areas of circles are proportional to the value of intraregional trade in 2010 that would be covered.
Source: Authors' illustration.

results will depend on whether the template adopted is based on the TPP, ASEAN+3, or a combination of the two. Alternative simulations are conducted on these options. In all cases the regionwide agreement is assumed to be reached in 2020, as articulated in APEC's Yokohama Vision (APEC 2010), and to be implemented over the next five years.

The rough economic scale of each track is illustrated in figure 3.2. Each grouping is represented by a circle with an area proportional to its intraregional trade in 2010. The Trans-Pacific track starts from a tiny circle (the P4) but expands rapidly with intraregional trade in the TPP13 reaching 41 percent of total FTAAP trade. The Asian track begins with a larger circle based on ASEAN, but even with enlargement into the ASEAN+3 it covers only 24 percent of the intraregional trade in the Asia-Pacific, since much of that takes place across the Pacific or in North America.

The model permits the simulation of a variety of scenarios beyond these prominent Trans-Pacific and Asian alternatives. For example, we have already examined a scenario that includes India in an eventual variant of the FTAAP. The scenarios examined so far are listed in table 3.1. Additional possibilities will also be examined from time to time and reported on our website, www. asiapacifictrade.org.

Table 3.1   Summary of scenarios

Scenario	Description	Parameter changes
Baseline	IMF/CEPII growth; implementation of agreed FTAs	Tariff and nontariff barrier (NTB) changes as scheduled
TPP track	TPP9 agreement and subsequent enlargement to TPP13	Tariff and NTB changes similar to those of prior agreements among TPP members; greater utilization of prior preferences due to cumulation of rules of origin (ROO)
Asian track	China-Japan-Korea agreement and subsequent ASEAN+3 FTA	Tariff and NTB changes similar to those of recent ASEAN agreements; increased utilization of prior preferences due to cumulation of ROO
FTAAP from TPP track	Enlargement of TPP track to cover all 21 APEC economies	Tariff and NTB reductions similar to TPP track; greater utilization of prior preferences due to cumulation of ROO
FTAAP from Asian track	Enlargement of Asian track to cover all 21 APEC economies	Tariff and NTB reductions similar to Asian track; greater utilization of prior preferences due to cumulation of ROO
FTAAP from both tracks	Consolidation of both tracks to cover all 21 APEC economies	Tariff and NTB reductions at average of TPP and Asian tracks; greater utilization of prior preferences due to cumulation of ROO
FTAAP with India	Enlargement of FTAAP from both tracks to include India	Tariff and NTB reductions similar to those of FTAAP from both tracks

Note: Additional scenarios to account for changing configurations of members and agreements will be calculated from time to time and reported on our website, www.asiapacifictrade.org.

Source: Authors' specification.

Simulating the Effects of Trade Agreements

The TPP and Asian tracks are simulated by implementing the sequences of trade agreements illustrated in figure 3.1. Each agreement is modeled by introducing changes in five sets of parameters that constitute the protection structure of the model:

- utilization rates of tariff preferences,
- tariffs,

- nontariff barriers,
- costs of rules of origin, and
- barriers to foreign direct investment.

These changes, in turn, are based on the actual or expected content of each agreement, including especially the scores of provisions on various issues. For prospective agreements, templates are estimated based on past agreements by the same principal parties. Thus, the TPP template was based on an average of five recent US agreements and the P4 agreement, and the China-Japan-Korea template was based on recent past templates used by the three countries. Larger Asian track agreements were based on recent ASEAN templates. This section outlines the methodology used to change parameters; further technical detail is provided in appendices D and E.

Utilization Rates of Tariff Preferences. Unlike much previous work, the simulations recognize that tariff preferences under FTAs are not fully utilized by the trade flows that they cover. Considerable empirical evidence suggests that observed utilization rates are typically far below unity (Kawai and Wignaraja 2011). This is partly due to economic causes—some trade flows may not satisfy an agreement's rules of origin. But it is also often due to administrative causes—exporters are not familiar with preferences, or certification costs are too high compared with benefits. Based on the results of empirical studies (Kawai and Wignaraja 2011, Athukorala and Kohpaiboon 2011), we model preference utilization as a function of the size of the preference margin and the size of agreements. We assume that large tariff preference margins and large-scale agreements make it more likely that the agreement will be utilized. The tariff reductions applied to trade flows are then calculated as the product of the preference utilization rate and the tariff reduction rate specified by an agreement.

Tariffs. Somewhat surprisingly, the tariff consequences of trade agreements are difficult to estimate. Base year information on tariffs is available in the GTAP dataset, but scheduled changes have to be derived from the detailed texts of trade agreements, which are difficult to process. Tariff schedules are usually expressed as detailed rules—say, tariffs for a certain group of Harmonized Schedule 8-digit trade classifications are reduced to no more than "20 percent in year one and 5 percent in year ten"—but the schedules do not contain related information on initial MFN rates, applied tariff rates, or trade weights that could be used for aggregation. Moreover, agreement texts are not stored or presented in a form that facilitates computer processing. So, while most of the data needed to calculate exact tariff schedules exist online, it would take a great deal of time and resources to process, combine, and harmonize these sources. We hope that such data consolidation efforts will be undertaken in the future; they would greatly facilitate the comparison and potential consolidation of bilateral and regional agreements. In lieu of such data sources, we had to make various approximations to estimate tariff reduction schedules.

Nontariff Barriers (NTBs). Lowering NTBs is an increasingly important goal of trade liberalization as tariff rates decline. We measure NTBs as tariff-equivalents—a wedge between the exporter's production costs and the importer's consumer prices—that result from regulations that raise production costs and create rents for importers, exporters, or both. We assembled estimates from several sources, allocated the estimates to production costs (50 percent), importer rents (25 percent), and exporter rents (25 percent), and applied reductions to these barriers based on the scores assigned to the relevant provisions of trade agreements. In the context of a heterogeneous firms model, we also had to judge whether reductions would apply to variable trade costs (associated with trading a unit of product) and/or fixed trade costs (associated with entering an export market). Our benchmark simulations assume that reductions apply to both types of impediments, but we also examined alternative assumptions in sensitivity experiments (see appendix F).

The size of the reductions in NTBs is determined from the scores that an agreement receives on provisions relevant to NTBs. For example, 10 of the 21 issues tracked in our NTB database were judged to be relevant to services NTBs, and the ASEAN-Australia-New Zealand Free Trade Agreement (AANZFTA) had an average policy score of 0.62 on these issues. We multiplied this score by 0.67, the share of services NTBs that we assumed could be affected by policy changes, yielding the barrier reduction factor of 0.41. This was the rate applied in five equal annual parts to services NTBs in the simulations of the AANZFTA.

Costs of Rules of Origin. In contrast to most previous work, we attributed productivity losses to the utilization of preferential trade agreements under rules of origin (ROO). The rationale for such an adjustment is that a producer may satisfy ROO by substituting costly domestic or regional inputs for less costly inputs from partners outside an FTA. (Another source of productivity losses is the administrative cost of the ROO certification process itself.) These efficiency losses were assumed to vary positively with the size of the preferential margin and negatively with the scale of the FTA. The resulting losses were added to "iceberg costs" associated with trade under a preferential agreement.

Investment Barriers. The reduction of investment barriers is a key objective of several agreements analyzed in this study. While FDI has been incorporated endogenously into some CGE studies, the many innovations already incorporated in the present model made it prudent to address FDI effects in a simpler form, as a separate side model. We began by constructing baseline projections of bilateral FDI stock matrixes over the 2010–25 period using a gravity model framework. We next estimated potential increases in inward FDI stocks, based on cross-country regression equations. We then determined to what extent the potential increases would be realized under particular agreements, given the scores of their investment provisions. The methodology used was similar to that applied to NTBs: An average score was calculated for provisions that affect investment for each agreement, and this score was multiplied by the share

Table 3.2   Assumptions about prospective agreements

| Agreement | Signed | In force | Intraregional exports | | Preference utilization rate | Reductions in 2025 | | | |
| | | | 2010 (billions of dollars) | Percent of 2010 total | | Final tariffs | Nontariff barriers | | | FDI barrier |
							Goods	Services		
TPP9	2013	2014	311	13.3	0.43	0.96	0.53	0.52	0.52
TPP13	2014	2015	1,977	46.6	0.58	0.96	0.53	0.52	0.52
China-Japan-Korea	2013	2014	607	21.3	0.53	0.92	0.37	0.35	0.35
ASEAN+3	2016	2017	1,341	32.5	0.60	0.90	0.36	0.28	0.28
TPP > FTAAP	2020	2021	4,797	67.3	0.67	0.96	0.53	0.52	0.52
Asia > FTAAP	2020	2021	4,797	67.3	0.67	0.90	0.36	0.28	0.28
Both > FTAAP	2020	2021	4,797	67.3	0.67	0.93	0.45	0.40	0.40
FTAAP+India	2020	2021	5,023	68.5	0.67	0.93	0.45	0.40	0.40

Source: Authors' estimates.

of investment barriers judged to be accessible to policy. The resulting "barrier reduction factor" was then used to simulate FDI changes. The benefits associated with these changes, which accrue in part to the host and in part to the investing country, were estimated using partial equilibrium welfare analysis. The methodology is explained in appendix E, and the results for groups of parameters are presented in table 3.2.

The various parameter changes developed in these five areas are presented in table 3.2 for the major prospective FTAs. But what if a bilateral trade flow is covered by several FTAs? For example, Japanese trade with Malaysia is already covered in the baseline scenario by a bilateral agreement between Japan and Malaysia and a general agreement between Japan and ASEAN. This same flow may eventually be covered also by an ASEAN+3 agreement and by a TPP track agreement. In such cases of overlapping rules, we calculated barriers for each type of transaction under each applicable agreement and then selected the one that offered that transaction the lowest possible barriers. In some cases, this meant, for example, that even if a new, larger agreement left tariffs unchanged, it might lower barriers because it would imply a higher preference utilization rate.

4

Economic Implications of the Trans-Pacific and Asian Tracks

The results suggest significant and widely distributed benefits from both tracks of agreements. They provide some surprises—mostly traceable to plausible features of the model and data—and also confirm expectations about how trade liberalization affects income and trade.

The most striking result is the sheer size of the predicted gains. By 2025, the TPP track would yield global annual benefits of $295 billion and the Asian track $500 billion. The benefits from regionwide free trade—the grand prize involving the consolidation of the tracks—would reach $1,922 billion, or 1.9 percent of world GDP. These numbers are large both absolutely and comparatively—for example, Gary Clyde Hufbauer and colleagues recently estimated the benefits from a Doha Development Agenda agreement in the $63 billion to $283 billion range.[1] And as we show, the gains are widely shared and result mainly from trade and investment creation, not diversion.

These and other quantitative estimates presented below are of course subject to considerable uncertainty and error. By analyzing related studies and conducting sensitivity analysis with the present model, in appendix F we attempt to provide more insight into the sources and interaction of possible errors. No precise error values can be calculated for the final estimate, but adding +/– 1/3 to specific income estimates would be very consistent with our sensitivity results.

---

1. These estimates are not directly comparable to the present results because they are not scaled to the economy of 2025; in percentage terms they range from 0.1 to 0.5 percent of world GDP (see Hufbauer, Schott, and Wong 2010). Some larger estimates are also reported in Fergusson (2008).

Some outcomes confirm well-known expectations about trade liberalization. The gains from liberalization, in percentage terms, are largest for smaller economies. The gains are also relatively large for economies with sizable initial barriers; the liberalizing home economy, rather than its foreign partners, gains the most from eliminating price distortions. Finally, liberalization amplifies trade and structural change based on comparative advantage—for example, it predicts strong gains for US services industries, which represent America's dominant area of comparative advantage.

Income Effects

Income gains are measured using the standard "equivalent variations" approach, which identifies the income required, at fixed prices but without an agreement, to match the real expenditure changes that result from an agreement. Income gains arise from various aspects of trade agreements that affect production, prices, and the variety of goods available to consumers and investors. A brief overview of the sources of gains measured in this study and their relative importance is provided in box 4.1.

The benefits of the TPP and Asian tracks are likely to appear slowly but should accelerate rapidly toward the end of our projection period (figure 4.1). The slow start is the outcome of the complexity of trade liberalization in the current environment; even under our optimistic assumptions the initial agreements will be relatively small, and their implementation will be gradual. Even given an optimistic schedule, the tracks will not generate benefits until 2014, when the first hypothetical TPP and China-Japan-Korea agreements would come into force, and in that year global benefits would be only $3 billion on the TPP track and $18 billion on the Asian track. (Benefits from other trade agreements already in effect are included in the baseline and are thus part of the "zero" axis in figure 4.1.)

From these modest beginnings, the benefits on the TPP and Asian tracks would rise rapidly to $232 billion and $251 billion, respectively, by 2020. The dashed lines then show what would happen if the tracks remain separate. Gains on the TPP track would grow to $295 billion with economic growth. Gains on the Asian track would increase more substantially to $500 billion, reflecting the somewhat later implementation of the ASEAN+3 agreement and the relatively rapid growth of Asian-track economies.

What could happen next is especially important. The expansion of either track into a regionwide agreement is shown by the solid lines past 2020 (see figure 4.1). These point to dramatically higher returns: Enlarging the TPP into the FTAAP would push global income gains to $2.4 trillion, and enlarging the ASEAN+3 into the FTAAP would yield gains of $1.3 trillion, both relative to a baseline of no new agreements. Not only are the income effects on both tracks large but so are the differences between them. These are due to the difference in the underlying templates, since the membership of the endpoint agreement (the FTAAP) and the timing of its implementation are assumed to be the

Box 4.1　How countries gain from trade liberalization

The list of sources of gains from trade has expanded substantially since David Ricardo (1817) pointed out that Portugal could benefit from trade by shifting workers into winemaking, its relatively high-productivity industry. In addition to intersectoral factor shifts, the potential gains addressed by our model include economies of scale, availability of more product varieties, changes in the proportion of productive firms within industries, and improvements in the terms of trade. The promotion of international investment, now also routinely included in trade agreements, provides still another source of benefits.

Table B4.1.1 separates total benefits into gains from FDI (as explained in appendix E), intensive margin trade, and extensive margin trade. Intensive margin trade effects—reflecting trade increases by already exporting firms—are similar to the benefits estimated in conventional general equilibrium models of liberalization. Extensive margin trade effects—reflecting exports by firms that did not serve a particular market before—provide additional gains that are unique to heterogeneous firm models. We estimate intensive margin benefits by running a simulation that liberalizes *only* variable cost (and not fixed cost) trade barriers. This eliminates most of the benefits gained from new entry (see also appendix F).[1] The difference between the total trade effects and those calculated in the intensive margin scenario are attributed to extensive margin trade.

Table B4.1.1　Income gains by type (percent)

Type	World	United States	China	Japan	Vietnam
			TPP track		
FDI effects	33.1	46.5	—	37.0	2.5
Intensive margin trade effects	23.2	10.1	—	21.9	54.2
Extensive margin trade effects	43.7	43.4	—	41.2	43.3
Total	100.0	100.0	—	100.0	100.0
			Asian track		
FDI effects	19.2	—	17.8	20.6	2.0
Intensive margin trade effects	37.5	—	37.2	36.5	72.9
Extensive margin trade effects	43.3	—	45.0	42.9	25.1
Total	100.0	—	100.0	100.0	100.0

Source: Authors' estimates.

(continued on next page)

1. This approach only approximates (actually sets an upper bound on) intensive margin effects, since even variable cost liberalization leads to some new entrants and hence extensive margin trade.

Box 4.1   How countries gain from trade liberalization *(continued)*

Extensive margin effects turn out to be the largest of the three types of gains on both tracks, accounting for 43 to 44 percent of total benefits. (This is consistent with the importance of the extensive margin trade in empirical studies of the effects of trade expansion, as reported, for example, by Hummels and Klenow [2005].) The next most important factor differs across agreements: For the TPP, it is investment liberalization, and for the Asian track, it is intensive margin trade. These results reflect differences in templates as well as the trade and investment patterns of the economies on the two tracks. For similar reasons, for the United States investment effects are most important, followed by extensive margin trade and then intensive margin trade. The ranking is reversed for Vietnam on both the TPP and Asian tracks. China and Japan fall in between.

Table B4.1.2 reports a second decomposition, showing trade changes by sector. The most striking result is that under the TPP the effects of liberalization are particularly concentrated on services; services account for a 32 percent increase in world exports but only 18 percent of baseline exports. The difference is especially large for the United States (64 percent share of export increases versus 33 percent baseline share). On the Asian track, by contrast, manufactures account for 80 percent of world export increases, compared with a 73 percent baseline share.

Table B4.1.2   Trade effects by sector (percent)

Sector	World	United States	China	Japan	Vietnam
	Share of 2025 baseline exports				
Primary products	9.4	7.9	0.1	0.2	9.6
Manufacturing	72.6	59.1	96.8	85.9	86.8
Services	18.0	33.0	3.1	13.9	3.6
Total	100.0	100.0	100.0	100.0	100.0
	TPP track share of export increase				
Primary products	−0.4	1.6	—	0.1	−4.0
Manufacturing	68.9	34.9	—	89.3	105.5
Services	31.5	63.5	—	10.5	−1.5
Total	100.0	100.0	—	100.0	100.0
	Asian track share of export increase				
Primary products	2.3	—	0.1	0.2	3.0
Manufacturing	80.4	—	96.4	85.4	97.9
Services	17.4	—	3.5	14.4	−0.8
Total	100.0	—	100.0	100.0	100.0

Source: Authors' estimates.

(continued on next page)

Figure 4.1   World income gains, 2010–25

billions of 2007 dollars

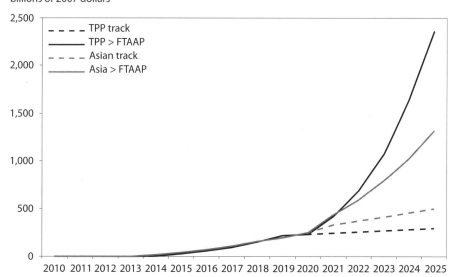

Source: Authors' estimates.

same regardless of the pathway used. The provisions of the TPP template yield
nearly twice the benefits that would be generated by an agreement covering
the same trade flows but based on the Asian template. The scale of both tracks,
the importance of regionwide consolidation, and the sensitivity of gains to the
template used are among the key findings of this study.

What would the agreements mean for particular countries? These results are reported in table 4.1 for 2025. In this and subsequent tables the scenarios appear as columns and the 24 countries and regions of the model are organized into four groups. The groups reflect assumptions about how different countries enter the scenarios. Specifically, (1) TPP track economies are countries that join *only* TPP track agreements, (2) Asian track economies are those that join *only* Asian track agreements, (3) two-track economies include those that join *both* TPP and Asian track agreements, and (4) the other group consists of economies involved in *neither* track (although some are part of the final FTAAP).

On the TPP track (second column of table 4.1), Japan and the United States would receive the largest absolute income gains, and Vietnam and Malaysia the largest percentage income gains. Korea and Mexico would also benefit substantially, despite the fact that both already have FTAs with the United States; their gains from the TPP track are attributable to new markets that will be covered by the agreement, including especially Japan. The results confirm expectations: Small and relatively protected economies have the largest percentage gains, but the gains reach across all participants and are relatively evenly distributed.

On the Asian track (third column of table 4.1), China, Japan, and Korea would be the largest absolute beneficiaries, and Hong Kong, Korea, and Vietnam would see the largest percentage gains. The gains of China, Japan, and Korea reflect in large part access to each others' markets, since they all already have bilateral FTAs with ASEAN. Hong Kong is projected to be a major beneficiary because it is both a service and investment hub (as shown below, much of its gains result from FDI effects), and it has not been fully integrated so far into the network of Asian FTAs. ASEAN would gain less from Asian track agreements than Northeast Asian economies because it already has bilateral agreements with China, Japan, and Korea. Indeed, results not shown in this table also indicate that ASEAN would suffer some trade diversion losses initially, as the China-Japan-Korea agreement is implemented.

The Asian track yields larger income gains than the TPP track. This is unexpected, because the Asian track covers less trade than the TPP track (see figure 3.2 in chapter 3) and is assumed to apply a less rigorous template. But Asian track economies have relatively high initial barriers, and there are no prior preferential agreements to blunt their impact on trade among the group's largest economies, China, Japan, and Korea. Thus, even a less rigorous template leads to substantial new integration. Of course, these same factors—high initial barriers and no prior agreements on Northeast Asian trade—also mean that progress on the Asian track will be harder and possibly slower.

If the TPP and Asian tracks progress in parallel but independently (fourth column of table 4.1), the gains will reach $766 billion, close to the sum of their separate effects. Because the tracks are structurally different—one includes the United States, the other China, and their templates cover different objectives—they provide mostly complementary benefits. The "two-track economies"

Table 4.1 Income gains under alternative scenarios

| Economy | GDP, 2025 (billions of 2007 dollars) | Income gains in 2025 (billions of 2007 dollars) | | | | Percent change from baseline | | | |
		TPP track	Asian track	Both tracks	FTAAP	TPP track	Asian track	Both tracks	FTAAP
TPP track economies	26,502	128.7	7.8	135.6	405.4	0.5	0	0.5	1.5
United States	20,273	77.5	2.5	79.6	266.5	0.4	0	0.4	1.3
Australia	1,433	8.6	0.2	8.8	26.4	0.6	0	0.6	1.8
Canada	1,978	9.9	0.4	10.3	26.2	0.5	0	0.5	1.3
Chile	292	2.6	0.1	2.7	6.5	0.9	0	0.9	2.2
Mexico	2,004	21.0	4.2	24.7	67.7	1.0	0.2	1.2	3.4
New Zealand	201	4.5	0.3	4.8	5.8	2.2	0.1	2.4	2.9
Peru	320	4.5	0.1	4.6	6.3	1.4	0	1.4	2.0
Asian track economies	20,084	−55.9	304.2	253.3	844.4	−0.3	1.5	1.3	4.2
China	17,249	−46.8	233.3	189.3	678.1	−0.3	1.4	1.1	3.9
Hong Kong	406	−0.8	42.7	42.0	84.9	−0.2	10.5	10.3	20.9
Indonesia	1,549	−3.5	12.8	10.1	38.0	−0.2	0.8	0.7	2.5
Philippines	322	−1.1	5.5	4.7	15.9	−0.3	1.7	1.5	4.9
Thailand	558	−3.7	9.9	7.2	27.4	−0.7	1.8	1.3	4.9
Two-track economies	8,660	245.9	210.7	420.3	483.4	2.8	2.4	4.9	5.6
Brunei	20	0.2	0.6	0.7	1.1	1.1	2.8	3.6	5.4
Japan	5,338	119.4	103.1	209.5	228.1	2.2	1.9	3.9	4.3
Korea	2,117	45.8	87.2	115.1	129.3	2.2	4.1	5.4	6.1

(continued on next page)

Table 4.1 Income gains under alternative scenarios (*continued*)

Economy	GDP, 2025 (billions of 2007 dollars)	Income gains in 2025 (billions of 2007 dollars)				Percent change from baseline			
		TPP track	Asian track	Both tracks	FTAAP	TPP track	Asian track	Both tracks	FTAAP
Two-track economies (continued)									
Malaysia	431	26.3	8.3	33.5	38.4	6.1	1.9	7.8	8.9
Singapore	415	8.1	–2.0	5.8	13.6	2.0	–0.5	1.4	3.3
Vietnam	340	46.1	13.5	55.8	72.9	13.6	4.0	16.4	21.5
Other	47,977	–24.0	–22.9	–43.5	188.6	0	0	–0.1	0.4
Russia	2,865	–2.0	–2.6	–4.2	265.9	–0.1	–0.1	–0.1	9.3
Taiwan	840	–2.9	–15.9	–17.6	53.0	–0.3	–1.9	–2.1	6.3
Europe	22,714	–3.4	4.7	1.1	–32.6	0	0	0	–0.1
India	5,233	–3.8	–7.9	–11.0	–29.5	–0.1	–0.2	–0.2	–0.6
Other ASEAN	83	–0.4	1.0	0.6	3.1	–0.5	1.1	0.7	3.7
Rest of world	16,241	–11.4	–2.0	–12.4	–71.4	–0.1	0	–0.1	–0.4
World	103,223	294.7	499.9	765.6	1,921.7	0.3	0.5	0.7	1.9
Memorandum									
TPP	35,162	374.6	218.5	555.9	888.8	1.1	0.6	1.6	2.5
ASEAN+3	28,828	189.5	515.9	674.1	1,330.8	0.7	1.8	2.3	4.6
APEC	58,951	313.7	504.2	787.3	2,052.0	0.5	0.9	1.3	3.5

Notes: The country groups correspond to membership assumptions used in different scenarios. "TPP track economies" participate only in Trans-Pacific track agreements. "Asian track economies" participate only in Asian agreements. "Two-track economies" participate in both sets of agreements. The FTAAP includes all of the above economies plus Russia, Taiwan, and Other ASEAN.

Source: Authors' estimates.

of our country classification scheme, those participating in both tracks, are projected to be the biggest winners under this scenario. Their income gains amount to 5 percent of their GDP compared with 0.5 percent for TPP track economies and 1.3 percent for Asian track economies. Indeed, two-track economies would capture 55 percent of the gains generated by the two tracks, even though they account for only 16 percent of the GDP of all participants.

The consolidation of the tracks into a regionwide agreement offers the most favorable outcomes. This scenario (fifth column of table 4.1) would produce gains of $1.9 trillion, far more than either track alone or even the two in parallel. This estimate is based on a consolidation reached from the TPP and Asian tracks through compromise; it uses a template that is the average of the TPP and Asian track templates. A stricter TPP template would yield even greater gains, as reported in table 5.3 in chapter 5. Economies that participate in only one track would be especially important gainers from consolidation: TPP and Asian track economies would roughly triple the gains that they could achieve on their own tracks. By contrast, economies that participate on both tracks and thus have access to both markets before consolidation would gain much less; for them, the FTAAP would add only 15 percent more income.

Trade and Investment Effects

Ambitious Asia-Pacific trade agreements would dramatically change world exports.[2] The effects would start small: In 2014 the TPP track would generate $9 billion and the Asian track $77 billion in additional exports. But by 2025 the projected increases on the TPP and Asian tracks grow to $444 billion and $945 billion, respectively, and $1.3 trillion together (table 4.2).

As with income, the Asian track would have a larger impact on trade than the TPP track, even though it covers less intraregional trade ($1.2 trillion versus $2 trillion). As already noted, Asian track economies have higher barriers to start. In contrast, the largest trade flows in the TPP—those among Canada, Mexico, and the United States, and between the United States and several partners—are already covered by high-quality FTAs. To the extent that the TPP contributes significant value, it will be in new areas such as services, IPRs, and investment.

On the TPP track, Japan and the United States would have the largest absolute export increases, and Vietnam, Japan, Malaysia, and Korea would have the largest percentage increases. On the Asian track, China, Japan, and Korea would have the largest gains; in percentage terms they would be joined by Hong Kong. ASEAN countries would gain much less because they already have preferential access to all ASEAN+3 markets. The export effects of both tracks moving forward would be similar to the sum of their separate impacts.

---

2. We report exports only. Given that the scenarios assume fixed capital account balances, the effects of scenarios on total exports and imports are similar. Results for imports will be available at our website, www.asiapacifictrade.org.

Table 4.2 Export increases under alternative scenarios

Economy	Exports, 2025 (billions of 2007 dollars)	Export increases in 2025 (billions of 2007 dollars)				Percent change from baseline			
		TPP track	Asian track	Both tracks	FTAAP	TPP track	Asian track	Both tracks	FTAAP
TPP track economies	4,555	201.5	0.5	199.5	779.9	4.4	0	4.4	17.1
United States	2,813	124.2	2.1	124.6	575.9	4.4	0.1	4.4	20.5
Australia	332	14.9	0.2	15.0	52.8	4.5	0.1	4.5	15.9
Canada	597	15.7	–1.4	14.2	32.0	2.6	–0.2	2.4	5.4
Chile	151	3.8	–0.9	2.9	8.2	2.5	–0.6	1.9	5.5
Mexico	507	31.5	0.4	31.3	94.3	6.2	0.1	6.2	18.6
New Zealand	60	4.7	0.1	4.8	6.0	7.8	0.1	8.0	9.9
Peru	95	6.7	0	6.6	10.0	7.1	0	7.0	11.3
Asian track economies	5,971	–73.8	618.4	544.1	1,772.2	–1.2	10.4	9.1	29.7
China	4,597	–57.4	516.3	456.8	1,505.3	–1.2	11.2	9.9	32.7
Hong Kong	235	–1.8	35.3	33.3	71.8	–0.8	15.0	14.2	30.6
Indonesia	501	–5.6	32.6	27.6	97.4	–1.1	6.5	5.5	19.5
Philippines	163	–1.9	8.8	7.1	27.2	–1.2	5.4	4.3	16.7
Thailand	476	–7.2	25.3	19.3	70.5	–1.5	5.3	4.0	14.8
Two-track economies	2,817	406.4	416.7	740.6	852.1	14.4	14.8	26.3	30.3
Brunei	9	0.3	0.3	0.5	0.6	2.8	3.5	5.9	7.0
Japan	1,252	175.7	220.7	364.5	423.1	14.0	17.6	29.1	33.8
Korea	718	88.7	168.3	220.4	245.2	12.4	23.4	30.7	34.1

Malaysia	336	41.7	12.4	51.3	50.8	12.4	3.7	15.3	15.1
Singapore	263	11.0	-9.0	1.3	-5.3	4.2	-3.4	0.5	-2.0
Vietnam	239	89.1	24.0	102.6	137.7	37.3	10.1	42.9	57.6
Other	15,072	-90.4	-90.2	-179.6	-53.5	-0.6	-0.6	-1.2	-0.4
Russia	1,071	-4.4	-4.0	-8.6	301.0	-0.4	-0.4	-0.8	28.1
Taiwan	712	-7.4	-37.7	-43.0	151.1	-1.0	-5.3	-6.0	21.2
Europe	7,431	-38.3	-28.3	-67.7	-268.2	-0.5	-0.4	-0.9	-3.6
India	869	-6.7	-7.5	-13.8	-44.7	-0.8	-0.9	-1.6	-5.1
Other ASEAN	34	-1.1	1.4	0.4	7.0	-3.2	4.3	1.1	20.8
Rest of world	4,955	-32.4	-14.2	-46.8	-199.7	-0.7	-0.3	-0.9	-4.0
World	28,415	443.7	945.4	1,304.6	3,350.7	1.6	3.3	4.6	11.8
Memorandum									
TPP	7,372	608.0	417.2	940.1	1,632.0	8.2	5.7	12.8	22.1
ASEAN+3	8,822	331.5	1,036.5	1,285.1	2,631.3	3.8	11.7	14.6	29.8
APEC	15,126	522.3	993.9	1,432.6	3,856.3	3.5	6.6	9.5	25.5

Source: Authors' estimates.

But again regionwide integration dominates the results. A comprehensive FTAAP would increase world exports twice as much as the TPP and Asian tracks independently, or by $3.3 trillion. These large gains—12 percent of baseline world exports—are much greater than those that might have resulted from the Doha Round.

Both tracks would make large contributions to FDI,[3] amounting to $560 billion on the two together (see table 4.3). The United States, Hong Kong,[4] and Japan are projected to have the largest gains in outward FDI. The model also generates rapid increases in outward FDI stocks for China, but these start from a low initial base. Also, Chinese foreign investments have historically targeted either countries outside the Asia-Pacific region or Asia-Pacific economies with low initial barriers to FDI (such as Australia, Canada, Hong Kong, and the United States). Hence the simulations of new regional agreements do not produce large absolute increases in China's outbound FDI. The projections are arguably more speculative for China than for other countries, given the dynamism of its transformation and potential changes in its investment patterns.

The TPP track would generate greater FDI impacts than the Asian track; TPP members play a large role in outward foreign investment and often face high barriers abroad. Furthermore, the TPP template is specifically designed to improve investment rules. Foreign investments in Japan and Korea are especially important in the projections, since their barriers to inward FDI are estimated to be high.

Structural Change

The tracks will also change what each economy produces (see table 4.4). Since manufacturing accounts for three-quarters of world trade, the largest effects, roughly two-thirds of export increases, would be in manufacturing. In proportional terms, however, services would gain more, and primary products less. Under the FTAAP, for example, services exports would increase by 18 percent, compared with 12 percent for manufactures and 3 percent for primary products.

The shifting composition of trade reflects several trends. The structure of demand is shifting toward services everywhere as incomes rise. Also, the rise of manufacturing trade in recent decades has been driven by sharp increases in import penetration rates, which are reaching such high levels that they are bound to slow. These historical increases in manufacturing import penetration have been driven by the dramatic rise of Chinese manufacturing

---

3. We report outward FDI stocks only. Results for inward stocks will be available at our website, www.asiapacifictrade.org.

4. Hong Kong is a major regional investment hub. As discussed in appendix E, this appears to be the case even though we have attempted to correct reported foreign investment data for "round tripping" of investments in China by Chinese firms through Hong Kong and for Hong Kong's role as a tax haven for foreign investment from other sources.

Table 4.3 Outward FDI stock increases under alternative scenarios

Economy	Outward FDI stock, 2025 (billions of 2007 dollars)	FDI stock increases in 2025 (billions of 2007 dollars)				Percent change from baseline			
		TPP track	Asian track	Both tracks	FTAAP	TPP track	Asian track	Both tracks	FTAAP
TPP track economies	10,980	190.9	0	190.9	540.9	1.7	0	1.7	4.9
United States	8,705	169.0	0	169.0	470.7	1.9	0	1.9	5.4
Australia	660	8.0	0	8.0	25.5	1.2	0	1.2	3.9
Canada	1,343	12.1	0	12.1	42.7	0.9	0	0.9	3.2
Chile	39	0.2	0	0.2	0.2	0.5	0	0.5	0.5
Mexico	199	0.8	0	0.8	0.8	0.4	0	0.4	0.4
New Zealand	29	0.7	0	0.7	0.8	2.4	0	2.4	2.9
Peru	7	0.1	0	0.1	0.1	1.6	0	1.6	1.7
Asian track economies	4,247	0	110.5	110.5	235.8	0	2.6	2.6	5.6
China	1,859	0	5.5	5.5	17.0	0	0.3	0.3	0.9
Hong Kong	2,171	0	98.3	98.3	204.4	0	4.5	4.5	9.4
Indonesia	44	0	0.6	0.6	1.2	0	1.4	1.4	2.8
Philippines	30	0	1.1	1.1	2.2	0	3.6	3.6	7.1
Thailand	143	0	4.9	4.9	11.0	0	3.4	3.4	7.7
Two-track economies	4,529	101.7	176.7	258.8	333.0	2.2	3.9	5.7	7.4
Brunei	22	0	1.4	1.4	2.6	0	6.2	6.2	11.9
Japan	2,172	74.1	111.5	171.2	198.4	3.4	5.1	7.9	9.1
Korea	607	11.3	59.6	66.2	78.0	1.9	9.8	10.9	12.8

(continued on next page)

Table 4.3   Outward FDI stock increases under alternative scenarios *(continued)*

Economy	Outward FDI stock, 2025 (billions of 2007 dollars)	FDI stock increases in 2025 (billions of 2007 dollars)				Percent change from baseline			
		TPP track	Asian track	Both tracks	FTAAP	TPP track	Asian track	Both tracks	FTAAP
Two-track economies (continued)									
Malaysia	388	3.5	4.2	7.2	12.3	0.9	1.1	1.9	3.2
Singapore	1,336	12.7	0	12.7	41.4	1.0	0	1.0	3.1
Vietnam	4	0	0	0	0.4	0.1	0.7	0.8	10.4
Other	33,055	0	0.2	0.2	45.2	0	0	0	0.1
Russia	883	0	0	0	32.3	0	0	0	3.7
Taiwan	330	0	0	0	12.5	0	0	0	3.8
Europe	27,737	0	0	0	0	0	0	0	0
India	298	0	0	0	0	0	0	0	0
Other ASEAN	5	0	0.2	0.2	0.4	0	3.6	3.6	6.9
Rest of world	3,802	0	0	0	0	0	0	0	0
World	52,812	292.6	287.4	560.4	1,154.9	0.6	0.5	1.1	2.2
Memorandum									
TPP	15,510	292.6	176.7	449.7	873.9	1.9	1.1	2.9	5.6
ASEAN+3	8,782	101.7	287.4	369.4	569.2	1.2	3.3	4.2	6.5
APEC	20,969	292.6	287.2	560.2	1,154.6	1.4	1.4	2.7	5.5

Source: Authors' estimates.

Table 4.4 Changes in world export composition under alternative scenarios

Sector	Exports, 2025 (billions of 2007 dollars)	Export increases in 2025 (billions of 2007 dollars)				Percent change from baseline			
		TPP track	Asian track	Both tracks	FTAAP	TPP track	Asian track	Both tracks	FTAAP
Primary products	2,670	–2	21	18	75	–0.1	0.8	0.7	2.8
Rice	20	0	0	0	0	0	1.5	1.4	2.1
Wheat	49	0	0	0	–1	–0.3	0.2	–0.2	–1.7
Other agriculture	806	0	11	11	53	0	1.4	1.4	6.6
Mining	1,796	–2	10	7	23	–0.1	0.5	0.4	1.3
Manufactures	20,637	306	760	994	2,372	1.5	3.7	4.8	11.5
Food and beverages	1,188	6	15	19	60	0.5	1.3	1.6	5.0
Textiles	735	29	45	69	132	3.9	6.2	9.3	17.9
Apparel and footwear	788	36	42	72	144	4.6	5.4	9.1	18.2
Chemicals	3,967	46	148	182	566	1.2	3.7	4.6	14.3
Metals	2,932	29	107	126	340	1.0	3.6	4.3	11.6
Electrical equipment	2,370	29	108	127	221	1.2	4.5	5.3	9.3
Machinery	4,093	46	180	210	414	1.1	4.4	5.1	10.1
Transportation equipment	2,806	56	56	107	232	2.0	2.0	3.8	8.3
Other manufactures	1,760	29	59	84	265	1.7	3.4	4.8	15.0

(continued on next page)

Table 4.4 Changes in world export composition under alternative scenarios *(continued)*

Sector	Exports, 2025 (billions of 2007 dollars)	Export increases in 2025 (billions of 2007 dollars)				Percent change from baseline			
		TPP track	Asian track	Both tracks	FTAAP	TPP track	Asian track	Both tracks	FTAAP
Services	5,108	140	164	292	904	2.7	3.2	5.7	17.7
Utilities	79	0	0	0	1	-0.1	0.3	0.1	0.9
Construction	171	3	6	9	39	1.7	3.4	5.3	22.5
Trade, transportation, and communications	2,017	61	99	152	430	3.0	4.9	7.5	21.3
Private services	2,356	73	55	126	403	3.1	2.4	5.3	17.1
Government services	484	2	4	6	31	0.5	0.8	1.2	6.5
Total	28,415	444	945	1,305	3,351	1.6	3.3	4.6	11.8

Source: Authors' estimates.

capabilities. While the projections anticipate some further deepening, they envision manufacturing export growth gradually settling back toward general economic growth. By contrast, the scope for deeper trade penetration in services remains very large. These shifts will also be encouraged by services-oriented liberalization, especially under the TPP.

On the TPP track, services trade would increase nearly twice as fast as manufactures, due to the factors noted above and the services-friendly template expected for the TPP. Even under the Asian track, however, services trade increases would nearly match those in manufacturing. Since services are also among the most protected sectors of the global economy, there are large opportunities to increase trade and related production efficiencies. Technological developments and new liberalization initiatives on both tracks will hopefully support these changes.

The same trends play out somewhat differently across economies, as illustrated by sectoral results for the United States, China, and Japan (figure 4.2). The figure shows how different sectors will be affected by regionwide integration under the TPP and Asian templates. The pattern of changes is similar across templates, driven by the underlying comparative advantages of the three economies. Both sets of bars show increases in US services value added (especially for private services) and to a lesser extent agricultural value added and declines in some manufacturing sectors. In China's case, the declines (of course, only relative to the baseline) appear primarily in services, while manufacturing value added would rise. Japanese results fall in between, with some services increases and a mixed pattern of changes in manufacturing. There are some notable differences between templates: The TPP template generates larger sectoral changes and more efficient specialization; in the United States, for example, this means more extensive shifts in value added from manufacturing to agriculture, food, and services.

These implications of the trade agreements can—and surely will—be presented in different ways. An interesting contrast is provided, for example, by pictures of Japanese production changes when measured in percentage terms (figure 4.3, graph A) and value terms (figure 4.3, graph B). The percentage measure draws attention to large declines in small sectors, mainly in agriculture, while the value-added measure draws attention to smaller percentage gains, which nevertheless add up to substantial benefits in large sectors such as services.

In a perfect world, trade agreements would strengthen economies across the board. This is true in a sense: The heterogeneous firms trade model predicts that liberalization will help to create pockets of productivity growth in all sectors of the economy, permitting incomes and wages to rise across the board. But benefits are still likely to have uneven sectoral effects, requiring workers and assets to shift among firms and sectors. In the case of the United States, relative to the baseline, resources will tend to move from manufacturing to services and primary products; in China, they will shift primarily from agriculture and services to manufacturing.

**Figure 4.2   Changes in value added in 2025: United States,
China, and Japan**

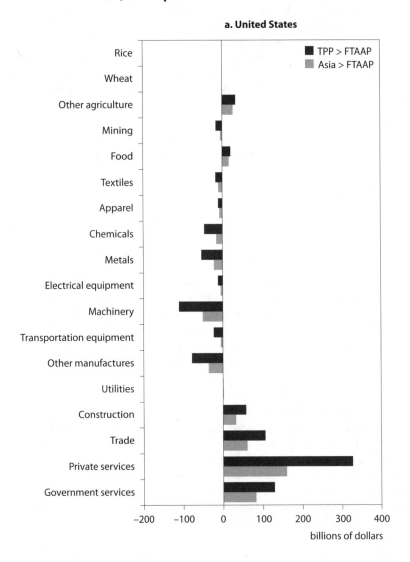

a. United States

billions of dollars

Figure 4.2 Changes in value added in 2025: United States, China, and Japan *(continued)*

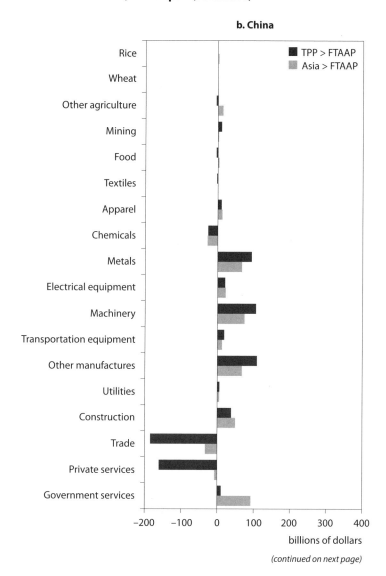

b. China

(continued on next page)

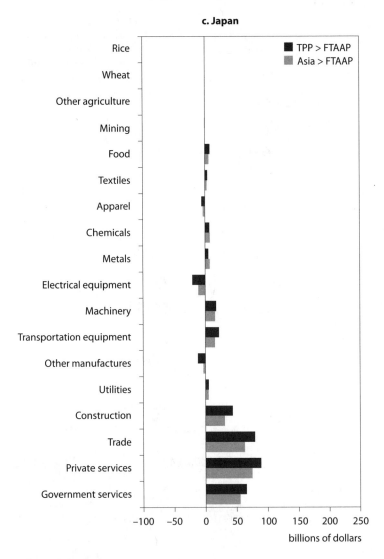

c. Japan

Source: Authors' estimates.

Figure 4.3 Two measures of Japanese output changes in 2025

a. In percent

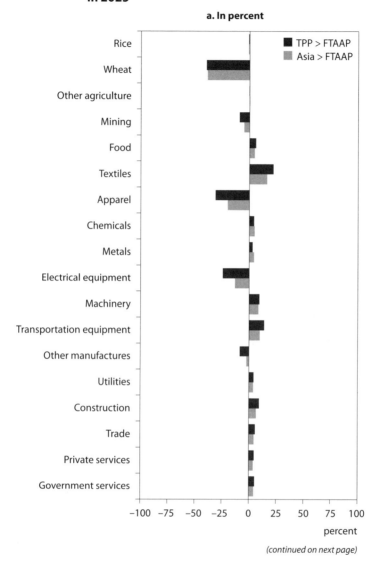

(continued on next page)

Figure 4.3   Two measures of Japanese output changes in 2025 *(continued)*

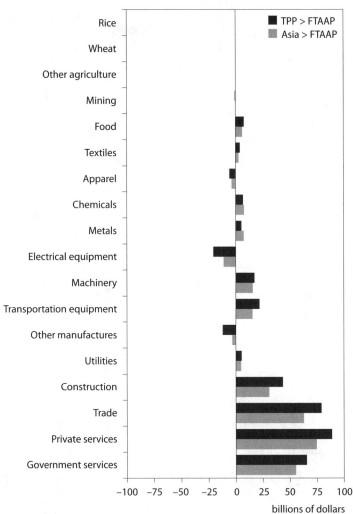

b. In billions of dollars

Source: Authors' estimates.

Intersectoral effects would emerge gradually. As examined further below, the annual adjustments are modest compared with underlying production activities. For example, even with ambitious regionwide trade agreements, there will be export *growth* in most US sectors, including manufacturing. The negative effects reported are relative to the baseline, and few imply actual declines over time. Moreover, the manufacturing-services distinction is itself becoming blurred. Manufacturing and services involve activities that may be reallocated, but most firms, industries, and workers are now typically involved in complex mixes of these activities. For example, firms such as Apple and IBM, once identified as manufacturers, thrive by shifting the mix of their activities into design and services and the management of international production chains. Indeed, the ability to shift costly activities abroad while producing high-quality products is itself a source of competitive advantage in advanced economies like the United States or Japan; it has enabled many companies to survive large technological and competitive challenges.

Employment Effects

The political debate about trade agreements, especially in the current macroeconomic climate, is likely to focus on employment effects. An agreement that is thought to contribute to unemployment will be politically unacceptable, whether or not it generates long-term benefits. Unfortunately, the trade-employment relationship is complicated and not well understood. For one thing, the relationship is very sensitive to underlying macroeconomic circumstances. The macroeconomic analysis of employment effects, in turn, requires very different models from those used to understand the microeconomics of international competition.

In CGE models, employment effects depend on the crucial "labor market closure" assumption made in solving the model. This assumption determines whether a change in net aggregate demand leads to changes in prices (wages and exchange rates) or to changes in quantities (employment and output). To model economies under conditions of unemployment, modelers usually assume that prices are fixed (say, in the short term for institutional reasons) and demand changes lead to employment and output changes. To model economies at full employment, they assume that the employment level is fixed and demand changes result in wage and real exchange rate adjustments (and hence real income changes). In the first case, benefits appear as output or employment gains; in the second, as income gains. For a given scenario and model, these two types of gains are closely related. For large economies, the output gains predicted by an unemployment closure roughly equal the income gains predicted by a full-employment closure.[5]

---

5. The unemployment model may then predict a larger or smaller final output effect depending on the Keynesian multiplier applied to the initial impact effect.

We use a full-employment specification in this study and therefore calculate income gains. We cannot predict the macroeconomic conditions many years into the future, when the full effects of trade agreements are likely to be felt; there is a much larger chance that the economy of 2025 will be near full employment than that it will be in recession. In any case, the rough equivalence of results between the closures implies that readers can translate income gains from our approach into employment gains in the alternative approach, simply by dividing by an employment/output ratio. Using US projections for 2025, one can calculate that the GDP of $20.3 trillion will be produced by 168 million workers; an income gain of $121,000 is roughly equivalent to creating an extra job.

Even under full employment, trade liberalization will change the sectoral composition of output and may require workers to shift from one industry to another. Such adjustments matter because they could generate private and social costs. When a worker loses a job, he or she may be forced to undertake a lengthy job search, learn a new skill, or move to a new location. It may also take public resources to manage these adjustments, and some older workers may even leave the labor force. At least in principle, measures of gains from trade should net out these adjustment costs.

The scale of the adjustment burden can be directly (although imperfectly) estimated from the annual results of the simulations. We define the "adjustment burden" of a growth path in year t as the sum of *reductions in employment* that occur in that year, summing across all sectors of the economy. Formally:

$$A_t^s = -\Sigma_i \min(0, L_{it}^s - L_{i,t-1}^s) \tag{4.1}$$

where A_t^s is the adjustment burden at time t under scenario s, and L_{it}^s is employment in sector i at time t under scenario s. In some of the calculations below the absolute adjustment burden defined by equation (4.1) is expressed as a percentage of total employment. Note that this calculation defines the adjustment burden in terms of intersectoral *job shifts*—the number of people who have to leave a sector and seek jobs in another—to distinguish it from macro-level employment effects that might or might not occur, depending on economic circumstances.

Adjustment burdens are a byproduct of economic change and emerge even on the baseline growth path. A sector's employment level will contract whenever its labor productivity outpaces the demand for output. In countries with high overall growth rates, all else equal, few sectors are likely to experience absolute employment declines and adjustment burdens will be low. But this is not an iron law: If rapid overall growth is associated with rapid productivity growth in a single, large sector with slowly growing demand (say, agriculture), then it will also result in high rates of adjustment. Adjustment burdens are much more likely to be large in countries with slow or even negative labor force growth, which implies slow demand growth and contracting employment in many sectors.

The negative relationship between adjustment burdens and baseline GDP growth is illustrated in figure 4.4. The left-most points show, based on the

Figure 4.4   Adjustment versus employment growth

adjustment burden (percent)

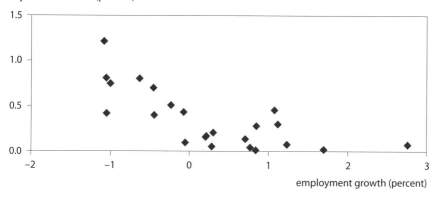

employment growth (percent)

Source: Authors' estimates.

Figure 4.5   Adjustment versus income gains from the FTAAP

job shifts (percent of employment)

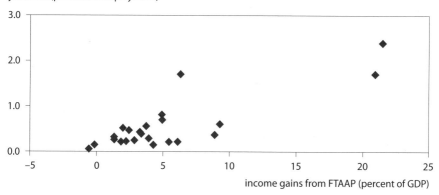

income gains from FTAAP (percent of GDP)

Source: Authors' estimates.

simulations, that adjustment burdens will be high (with total sectoral job losses of around 1 percent of total employment) in countries with employment growth in the low –1 percent range, such as Korea, Taiwan, and Russia.

Does trade liberalization impose large adjustment burdens? The answer will depend, of course, on the country, agreement, and point in time; implications for the United States will be examined in the next section. But the overall relationship that emerges from the simulations, illustrated in figure 4.5, is encouraging. This scatter diagram shows job shifts predicted by the simulations (vertical axis, as a percent of employment) against income gains predicted under the FTAAP scenario (horizontal axis, as a percent of GDP) for 22 countries and regions. It suggests a clear correlation between benefits and adjustment; income gains of 10 percent of GDP require that approximately 1 percent of the labor force change jobs.[6] The US example will also confirm this high ratio of returns to adjustment. Further, the adjustment burdens calculated in this study end once an economy completes its transition to a new trade structure, while the stream of income gains continues indefinitely into the future.

Impacts on Nonmembers

The results of the tracks show mostly gains, but negative effects appear for some countries (tables 4.1 and 4.2). These reflect the well-known trade diversion effects of free trade agreements: Preferences cause imports to shift from efficient, nonparticipating exporters to FTA partners that receive them. Trade diversion harms both the importer, which now pays more (net of tariffs), and the exporter, which suffers deterioration in its terms of trade, leading to wider welfare losses. In table 4.1, such losses appear for "Asian track" countries under the TPP scenario and for "other" countries under most scenarios.

The trade diversion effects of the TPP fall mainly on China—its exports would be 1.2 percent lower than on the baseline (table 4.2). The income implications are smaller, at around 0.3 percent of GDP (table 4.1). These effects mirror the gains of TPP members, such as Vietnam, that compete with China for US markets. Although the results show trade diversion also for TPP track economies under Asian track trade agreements, the income effects would be slightly positive. In that case, productivity gains appear to be large enough to improve the terms of trade for nonparticipating countries such as the United States, offsetting trade diversion losses. Thus, outsiders will likely capture some part of the benefits of Asian integration.

Not surprisingly, trade diversion losses are greatest for economies that participate in neither track. For example, Russia and Taiwan would experience losses under both tracks, in which they are assumed not to participate. These two economies, however, would have large gains from the FTAAP, since both are APEC members and are therefore assumed to participate. This example illustrates the importance of the membership assumptions built into our scenarios. The lists of participants in the various groups are far from certain, and membership decisions will depend on how countries expect to be affected by the evolving agreements.

---

6. The measure of job shifts used in this study accounts for intersectoral job shifts but not shifts within model sectors. It is therefore sensitive to sector detail; a model with 200 sectors would show more adjustment than one with 20. To be sure, shifts among the smaller subsectors of a large sector may involve lower adjustment costs because skill and location requirements may be more similar. Still, due to aggregation issues, our estimates may somewhat understate the extent of job shifts.

The implications for the European Union are especially interesting, since these might affect the global consequences of the tracks. The European Union has recently prioritized FTAs with Asia-Pacific economies; for example, it has concluded an FTA with Korea and has begun negotiations with ASEAN. The European Union is also discussing negotiations with the United States. These initiatives have been stimulated, in part, by increasing discrimination against Europe in Asia-Pacific markets. Our results do not suggest that the European Union would be much affected by Asia-Pacific preferential agreements; for example, the negative income effect of the TPP on Europe is estimated to be only $3 billion in 2025, in the context of a $23 trillion economy. The Asian track would actually yield a small *increase* in European incomes. But forgoing the potential positive benefits of membership in one or both tracks could be costly; we expect that the European Union will watch the negotiations carefully and may react to them. It might, for example, propose an early effort to transform the regional negotiations into a new global round.

Importantly, trade creation benefits vastly exceed trade diversion losses. For example, under the FTAAP, when approached from both tracks, members would gain $2,052 billion, while excluded regions (Europe, India, and the rest of the world) would lose $134 billion; this implies that trade diversion losses account for only 7 percent of the benefits. Comparable ratios for the TPP and Asian tracks are 21 and 4 percent, respectively. The reason trade diversion is so limited is that both tracks are close to "natural blocs," in that member economies already trade intensively with each other and each group comprises globally efficient producers for a wide range of products (Frankel, Stein, and Wei 1995). Liberalization also increases productivity in member economies and encourages further expansion of trade. Moreover, the large ratio of gains to diversion losses means that the participants will have resources available to blunt the negative impact of FTAs on excluded partners such as India and lower-income countries.

5

Dynamics of the Trans-Pacific and Asian Tracks

The rules of the Asia-Pacific economic system are the results of a "game"—that is, interdependent decisions by several countries. Once the TPP and Asian tracks are in motion, they will change the incentives that face current and potential members in making decisions about whether or not to participate in one or both tracks. Overall, these changes suggest that each track will generate incentives for enlargement and stimulate progress on the other. The mutual development of the tracks, in turn, is likely to create incentives for consolidation.

The grand prize of the game is the estimated $1.9 trillion gain generated by the regionwide FTAAP in 2025 (see table 4.1 in chapter 4). Such a large surplus invites competition for shares—a reason for the "contest of templates" to develop rules that tilt benefits in favor of one or another group of countries. If disagreements about templates—representing the interests of countries and of industries and interest groups within them—are intense enough, they could make it impossible to reach an agreement at all, despite the large potential benefits.

Because of such potentially destructive competition, smaller agreements among fewer, relatively compatible partners are more viable than larger, more profitable deals. Baldwin (1995, 2006) and McCulloch and Petri (1997) provide formal models to explain how such smaller deals might lead to sequential steps toward deeper liberalization. The TPP and Asian tracks might well be examples of such a process. If this is the case, the step-wise approach represented by regional agreements would not require sacrificing the end goal of regionwide integration; it would merely provide a feasible strategy for reaching it.

Trans-Pacific Track

Results for the TPP track show global benefits rising from $28 billion in 2015 to $232 billion in 2020 and $295 billion in 2025 (table 5.1). Early on, the main attraction of the track is preferential access to US markets. US import and investment barriers are generally low, but pockets of protection remain—for example, high tariffs on apparel. Reductions in these barriers may not justify a shift to US products but can give an advantage to economies like Vietnam, Malaysia, and Mexico that compete with China and other current suppliers outside the TPP. The preferences will not be large enough to offset large productivity gaps, but some of the affected industries are already looking for alternative production locations due to rising costs in China. The smaller countries that benefit from these trends will have powerful incentives to help get the TPP off the ground. Moreover, the investment protections offered by the TPP could reinforce these developments by stimulating FDI in expanding industries.

In the second stage, as the TPP expands to include Japan and Korea, the gains become larger and more widely distributed. Since the TPP will liberalize services and investment in these economies, their entry will generate significant effects in those sectors. Moreover, since Japan and Korea do not have an FTA with each other and other TPP partners, significant benefits will be generated in markets other than those of the United States. This stage is projected to lead to increased foreign investments among the United States, Japan, and Korea, accounting for a significant increase in projected benefits—a nearly tenfold increase in gains over the 2015–20 period. This second stage will add new "cylinders" to the TPP engine and should help to establish the track as a major fixture in the global trading system. The benefits will generate incentives for other countries to join and perhaps also acceleration on the Asian track.

After the second-stage agreements are implemented (in 2020 under our assumptions), the gains from the track will increase by a more moderate 27 percent in 2020–25. Losses to economies not participating in the track (particularly China) will become more apparent. Since similar patterns are also likely to emerge on the Asian track, the next logical set of opportunities involves the consolidation of the tracks into a regionwide or perhaps global agreement.

Asian Track

Results for the Asian track show benefits rising from $42 billion in 2015 to $251 billion in 2020 and $500 billion in 2025 (table 5.2). As with the TPP track, the dynamics of this path can be decomposed into three stages. The first stage focuses on the implementation of the China-Japan-Korea agreement. Most of the gains from this agreement would accrue to the three member countries, with approximately half going to China and the other half split nearly evenly between Japan and Korea. The estimated benefits for Korea are larger than those from the TPP track, mainly because Korea already has an FTA with the

Table 5.1 Income gains on the TPP track

Economy	Income gains in 2025 (billions of 2007 dollars)			Percent change from baseline		
	2015	2020	2025	2015	2020	2025
TPP track economies	10.7	97.3	128.7	0.1	0.4	0.5
United States	7.8	58.8	77.5	0	0.3	0.4
Australia	0.4	6.1	8.6	0	0.5	0.6
Canada	0.5	7.8	9.9	0	0.4	0.5
Chile	0	1.8	2.6	0	0.7	0.9
Mexico	1.4	16.4	21.0	0.1	1.0	1.0
New Zealand	0.4	3.2	4.5	0.3	1.8	2.2
Peru	0.2	3.3	4.5	0.1	1.3	1.4
Asian track economies	−2.9	−34.2	−55.9	0	−0.2	−0.3
China	−2.4	−27.6	−46.8	0	−0.2	−0.3
Hong Kong	−0.1	−0.6	−0.8	0	−0.2	−0.2
Indonesia	−0.2	−2.4	−3.5	0	−0.2	−0.2
Philippines	−0.1	−0.9	−1.1	−0.1	−0.4	−0.3
Thailand	−0.2	−2.7	−3.7	−0.1	−0.6	−0.7
Two-track economies	21.8	186.3	245.9	0.3	2.4	2.8
Brunei	0	0.2	0.2	0.1	0.9	1.1
Japan	12.9	95.5	119.4	0.3	1.9	2.2
Korea	3.5	34.9	45.8	0.2	2.0	2.2
Malaysia	2.7	19.2	26.3	1.0	5.6	6.1
Singapore	0	5.6	8.1	0	1.7	2.0
Vietnam	2.7	30.9	46.1	1.8	13.6	13.6
Other	−1.8	−17.5	−24.0	0	0	0
Russia	−0.1	−1.1	−2.0	0	−0.1	−0.1
Taiwan	−0.1	−2.1	−2.9	0	−0.3	−0.3
Europe	−0.6	−3.7	−3.4	0	0	0
India	−0.2	−2.3	−3.8	0	−0.1	−0.1
Other ASEAN	0	−0.3	−0.4	−0.1	−0.5	−0.5
Rest of world	−0.8	−7.9	−11.4	0	−0.1	−0.1
World	27.7	232.0	294.7	0	0.3	0.3
Memorandum						
TPP	32.4	283.6	374.6	0.1	0.9	1.1
ASEAN+3	18.8	151.8	189.5	0.1	0.7	0.7
APEC	29.3	246.2	313.7	0.1	0.5	0.5

Source: Authors' estimates.

Table 5.2 Income gains on the Asian track

Economy	Income gains in 2025 (billions of 2007 dollars)			Percent change from baseline		
	2015	2020	2025	2015	2020	2025
TPP track economies	0.7	3.3	7.8	0	0	0
United States	0	0.3	2.5	0	0	0
Australia	0	0	0.2	0	0	0
Canada	0	0.1	0.4	0	0	0
Chile	0	−0.1	0.1	0	0	0
Mexico	0.7	2.8	4.2	0	0.2	0.2
New Zealand	0	0.1	0.3	0	0.1	0.1
Peru	0	0.1	0.1	0	0	0
Asian track economies	13.5	132.7	304.2	0.1	0.9	1.5
China	15.2	113.3	233.3	0.2	0.9	1.4
Hong Kong	−0.1	16.1	42.7	0	4.8	10.5
Indonesia	−0.4	1.6	12.8	−0.1	0.1	0.8
Philippines	−0.3	0.9	5.5	−0.2	0.4	1.7
Thailand	−0.8	0.7	9.9	−0.2	0.2	1.8
Two-track economies	30.2	129.2	210.7	0.4	1.7	2.4
Brunei	0	0.2	0.6	0	0.9	2.8
Japan	16.8	68.2	103.1	0.4	1.4	1.9
Korea	14.5	58.9	87.2	1.0	3.4	4.1
Malaysia	−0.4	1.7	8.3	−0.2	0.5	1.9
Singapore	−0.3	−2.1	−2.0	−0.1	−0.6	−0.5
Vietnam	−0.3	2.3	13.5	−0.2	1.0	4.0
Other	−2.7	−14.1	−22.9	0	0	0
Russia	−0.4	−1.7	−2.6	0	−0.1	−0.1
Taiwan	−1.9	−9.4	−15.9	−0.4	−1.4	−1.9
Europe	0.2	1.4	4.7	0	0	0
India	−0.3	−2.6	−7.9	0	−0.1	−0.2
Other ASEAN	0	0.2	1.0	0	0.4	1.1
Rest of world	−0.4	−2.0	−2.0	0	0	0
World	41.7	251.0	499.9	0.1	0.3	0.5
Memorandum						
TPP	30.9	132.4	218.5	0.1	0.4	0.6
ASEAN+3	43.7	262.0	515.9	0.3	1.2	1.8
APEC	42.1	254.0	504.2	0.1	0.5	0.9

Source: Authors' estimates.

United States. The estimated benefits for Japan are roughly the same on both tracks. Overall, all three countries have strong incentives to move forward with the China-Japan-Korea agreement; the projected gains amply justify the vigorous efforts that leaders appear to be making to launch the negotiations. Of course, the political challenges for such an agreement are immense, spanning bitter historical memories, lingering tensions on territorial claims, and substantial differences in political philosophy. Moreover, there are large overlaps among the current and expected comparative advantages of the three countries, leading to substantial, industry-specific concerns in each.

In the period between the implementation of the China-Japan-Korea agreement and an ASEAN+3 agreement, other countries in the region would experience small and mostly negative spillovers. In 2015, for example, our Asian track results show negative effects for all other Asian economies except Brunei. The reason is that the China-Japan-Korea agreement would erode the preferential margins that ASEAN countries now enjoy in their FTAs with all three Northeast Asian partners. The losses, however, are small, in the range of 0.1 to 0.2 percent of GDP.

The second stage of the Asian track assumes the consolidation of existing agreements into a comprehensive ASEAN+3 agreement. We assume that this decision is concluded in 2016 and implemented over 2017–22. The major gainers would still be China, Japan, and Korea (accounting for 85 percent of Asian track gains in 2025). But by the end of this period, the early losses would turn to positives for all Asian economies, with the exception of Singapore. Singapore is unusual: It has very open markets and hence cannot gain from further liberalizing its imports, and it has a large initial portfolio of high-quality FTAs. The value of this portfolio would be eroded by preferences that the Asian track makes available to other Asian economies.

The development of the ASEAN+3 itself would offer moderate incremental gains, because all trade under an ASEAN+3 agreement would have been covered by the China-Japan-Korea agreement or existing ASEAN+1 agreements. The one important difference is that an ASEAN+3 agreement would be likely to allow—according to our assumptions—the cumulation of rules of origin across the entire region. This means that more trade will qualify for preferences, leading to a higher utilization of preferences and hence more trade. Our results suggest that this innovation will be important enough to yield gains of around 2 percent of GDP to ASEAN economies.

As on the TPP track, the growth of benefits would then slow. From the perspective of the Asian track too, the consolidation of the TPP and Asian tracks would offer the next logical opportunity for significant gains.

Pathways to Regionwide Agreements

A consistent theme of the results is that Asia-Pacific-wide integration could generate large benefits in the $1.3 trillion to $2.4 trillion range (table 5.3). Where an agreement falls in this range will depend on its template, or the

Table 5.3 Pathways to the FTAAP

Economy	GDP, 2025 (billions of 2007 dollars)	Income gains in 2025 (billions of 2007 dollars)			Percent change from baseline		
		Via TPP track	Via Asian track	Via an average of tracks	Via TPP track	Via Asian track	Via an average of tracks
TPP track economies	26,502	491.7	245.9	405.4	2.1	1.1	1.7
United States	20,273	328.2	166.6	266.5	1.8	0.9	1.5
Australia	1,433	32.5	15.3	26.4	2.6	1.2	2.1
Canada	1,978	31.4	14.3	26.2	1.8	0.8	1.5
Chile	292	8.6	2.2	6.5	3.6	0.9	2.7
Mexico	2,004	76.3	43.0	67.7	4.7	2.6	4.1
New Zealand	201	6.9	2.0	5.8	3.9	1.1	3.2
Peru	320	7.7	2.5	6.3	3.2	1.0	2.6
Asian track economies	20,084	1,082.5	628.6	844.4	7.5	4.4	5.9
China	17,249	837.1	520.6	678.1	6.8	4.3	5.5
Hong Kong	406	118.8	51.6	84.9	35.8	15.5	25.6
Indonesia	1,549	60.3	26.1	38.0	5.4	2.3	3.4
Philippines	322	22.5	11.2	15.9	8.9	4.4	6.3
Thailand	558	43.7	19.2	27.4	10.1	4.4	6.3
Two-track economies	8,660	519.6	306.2	483.4	6.8	4.0	6.3
Brunei	20	1.4	0.6	1.1	8.2	3.7	6.3
Japan	5,338	233.1	154.2	228.1	4.7	3.1	4.6
Korea	2,117	132.7	97.7	129.3	7.7	5.6	7.5

Malaysia	431	44.7	16.5	38.4	13.0	4.8	11.2
Singapore	415	26.5	-0.7	13.6	7.9	-0.2	4.0
Vietnam	340	81.1	37.9	72.9	35.8	16.8	32.2
Other	47,977	264.7	134.3	188.6	0.7	0.3	0.5
Russia	2,865	339.5	199.3	265.9	15.0	8.8	11.8
Taiwan	840	83.8	30.5	53.0	12.3	4.5	7.8
Europe	22,714	-40.9	-23.9	-326.0	-0.2	-0.1	-0.2
India	5,233	-37.1	-20.6	-29.5	-1.0	-0.6	-0.8
Other ASEAN	83	4.6	2.4	3.1	7.5	3.9	5.1
Rest of world	16,241	-85.2	-53.4	-71.4	-0.6	-0.4	-0.5
World	103,223	2,358.5	1,315.1	1,921.7	2.7	1.5	2.2
Memorandum							
TPP	35,162	1,011.3	552.2	888.8	2.9	1.6	2.5
ASEAN+3	28,828	1,606.7	937.3	1,330.8	7.3	4.2	6.0
APEC	58,951	2,517.1	1,410.7	2,052.0	5.2	2.9	4.2

Source: Authors' estimates.

pathway used to reach it; the TPP and Asian templates would provide different standards and favor different sectors.

What difference will the template make? To answer this question, we examined three alternative simulations of the FTAAP, based on the TPP template, the Asian track template, and a compromise between the two. The templates differ in many details, but generally the TPP provides more comprehensive tariff reductions, more ambitious cuts in NTBs, and more specific provisions to promote investment, services, and IPRs. These provisions benefit advanced countries but also yield increased trade and generate greater income gains for all countries. The definitions of the templates in terms of structural parameters are reported in table 3.2 in chapter 3.

Not surprisingly, the largest gains obtain from the most rigorous of the templates—the TPP pathway (table 5.3). This scenario generates benefits of $2.4 trillion, more than $1 trillion greater than the Asian pathway. The hybrid template, reached by merging the two pathways (in technical terms, by averaging the scores of the provisions of the two templates), would generate intermediate gains of $1.9 trillion. In all three cases, China and the United States would see large benefits, roughly tripling their income gains from the TPP and Asian agreements.

The United States would get a larger share of total benefits under the TPP rather than the Asian template (13 versus 12 percent), and China would get a larger share of benefits under the Asian rather than TPP template (40 versus 35 percent). In other words, the templates appear to be "doing the job" for their leading economies; the Asian template increases China's share, and the TPP template increases America's share. But the real message of table 5.3 is that share differences are *not* what matter—the depth of liberalization, and not its structure, dominates the gains. For example, while China gets a smaller share of the gains under the TPP, its absolute gains would be larger because the template generates greater overall benefits. Specifically, China's gains would be $317 billion or 61 percent higher with the TPP template than with an Asian template.

All participating countries would gain more under the TPP template than the Asian template, but the difference between these alternatives—the effects of using a "21st century template"—varies by economy. For example, Hong Kong and Singapore would especially benefit from the TPP approach, due to their large services and investment sectors. For Singapore, the TPP template would in fact turn small losses into a large gain. Russia and Korea, which are connected to the region's markets more through goods than services, would see smaller benefits from the TPP template.

Importantly, the pathways may also influence the probability of reaching a regionwide agreement. On one hand, the larger gains promised by the TPP template should provide stronger incentives for regionwide liberalization. On the other hand, the less demanding template of the Asian track—including the possibility of excluding sensitive sectors—could make it easier to reach a large agreement. To be sure, advanced economies like the United States and Singapore will no doubt hold out for provisions that favor their most competitive sectors.

Templates matter. The results suggest that the most important contribution that the TPP could make to the Asia-Pacific integration process might be its rigorous template, as a benchmark for future agreements. If a TPP-style template is adopted across the Asia-Pacific, it would add benefits of more than $1 trillion. Even if the template is only partially accepted because compromises dilute some of its provisions, it could still enhance the standards of a consolidated agreement. These incremental benefits would be widely shared, with most additional benefits flowing to Asian economies ($669 billion, or 64 percent of the world total). The indirect benefits of the TPP, as it raises standards for future agreements, could be much greater than the direct benefits it delivers through early-stage agreements.

Who Will Lead?

Trade agreements happen because of leadership. In the first stage of the tracks, the markets of China and the United States are likely to drive integration. Thus, initially, leadership is likely to come from these countries in partnership with smaller economies that can benefit from their markets. The P4 economies and the ASEAN economies have played the latter role in the case of the TPP and Asian tracks, respectively. China and the United States have so far provided leadership, even though their direct gains are likely to be modest. Their motivation is to promote templates that strengthen their key industries, alongside political benefits.

The region's middle-tier economies, including especially Japan and Korea, are critical to the second stage of development of the tracks. At this stage, the China-Japan-Korea agreement is the essential next step on the Asian track. The participation of Japan and Korea would also enhance the scope of the TPP, helping to generate momentum and perhaps more widely distributed leadership. Individual ASEAN economies and the Association itself may become more strongly engaged in order to ensure ASEAN's centrality in Asian integration. In this stage, more economies in the region may attempt to participate on both tracks, as Brunei, Malaysia, Singapore, and Vietnam are already doing.

With both tracks established and probably enlarged, it would again be up to China and the United States to complete the Trans-Pacific integration process. Economies that joined both tracks would have little to gain from further integration. Japan and Korea, for example, would have achieved 92 and 89 percent, respectively, of the potential gains from a regionwide FTAAP simply by joining both the TPP and Asian tracks (table 4.1). Indeed, a potential concern is that the "two-track economies" will slow the process of further integration or at least exert leverage to extract much of the incremental benefits. At the same time, the two-track economies will have expertise in dealing with both types of agreements and incentive to harmonize their provisions, so they could make valuable contributions to the consolidation effort.

In any case, the evolution of the tracks will substantially change the trading environment facing China and the United States. These two countries will have opened their markets to most other Asia-Pacific economies but not to each other. Consequently, moving to an FTAAP would mainly (and dramatically) increase their mutual gains. Once both tracks are fully established, moving to the FTAAP would multiply US income gains by a factor of 3.3 and China's benefits by a factor of 3.6 (table 4.1).

That China and the United States—the world's two largest economies, with roughly similar GDPs 15 years from now—will have to lead the last stage of Trans-Pacific integration is hardly surprising. Indeed, their interests in the TPP and Asian tracks already represent efforts to influence the eventual regional or even global trading system. This contest of templates defines what bargaining theory calls the "disagreement point" in negotiations, representing each party's payoff in the absence of an agreement. Theory suggests that the stronger disagreement point leads to a larger share of gains from a successful deal. This explains why each country is working hard to improve its fallback point. The results show that no matter how aggressively this disagreement point is developed—in other words, regardless of the success of the TPP and Asian track agreements—it will still yield benefits that fall far short of the gains from Pacific-wide free trade. In other words, it will create large incentives for a deal.

6

National Economic Interests

It is often said that all politics is local. The regional initiatives examined in this study will also have to pass the test of local politics in several countries. We briefly examine the effects on participating countries beginning with the region's three largest economies (the United States, China, and Japan) and then moving on to selected issues for other countries.[1] Our discussion remains focused on economic issues, but clearly the decisions countries make will also be based on politics. The agreements are already attracting opposition in many countries; "getting to yes" cannot be taken for granted in any country. We do not attempt an exhaustive analysis of these issues, but box 6.1 provides a sampling of emerging political debates.

United States

In the two decades since NAFTA and the Uruguay Round negotiations, the United States has signed few new trade agreements and provided limited support to the Doha Round. The domestic politics of trade policy has become highly controversial, even though it is one of the few areas of policy that can still attract bipartisan support in Congress. In the policy community, there is growing concern that the United States will fall behind East Asia and Europe in deepening its external linkages (Bergsten and Schott 2010). The TPP represents a more active US strategy, designed to develop high-quality rules, attract a critical mass of partners, and eventually extend high-standard rules to the

---

1. Detailed results for all countries and regions will be available at our website, www.asiapacific trade.org.

Box 6.1   Getting to yes: Domestic politics and the TPP

Trade liberalization generates widely distributed gains, but its costs often impact relatively few firms, industries, or localities. While the many recipients of gains have modest individual incentives to support an agreement, the few firms and workers that expect to be hurt are highly motivated to oppose it. The TPP too is likely to face powerful political headwinds in most participating countries. A partial list of examples from four selected countries follows.

In the United States (as elsewhere) the most contentious issue is likely to be copyright enforcement, with strong interest groups on both sides. Copyright-based industries argue for provisions that would go beyond the international Anti-Counterfeiting Trade Agreement (ACTA), while internet users and service providers strongly oppose such rules. The automobile industry supports the agreement but is strongly opposed to including Japan; it has called for commitments on US access to Japanese markets before Japan joins the negotiations. The textile and apparel industry forcefully argues for "yarn forward," a rule that would limit TPP preferences to those garments produced in Vietnam (and possibly other countries) that use US or other regional fabrics. State and local governments—presumably with support from states-rights activists—will oppose a government procurement chapter that goes beyond covering tenders from the federal government. Numerous civil society groups argue for greater public health exemptions from intellectual property protection for pharmaceuticals. Labor and environmental groups are watching closely; the US-Colombia FTA was held up due to alleged labor rights violations. Meanwhile, the business community strongly supports a positive outcome, and general public awareness is low.

Vietnam's political system differs from that of the United States but domestic issues will also have a large impact there. State-owned enterprises play an important role in the economy and could face significant adjustments under the competition policy chapter. (Singapore's large government-owned investment company Temasek has also opposed additional disclosure rules.) Labor provisions calling for "freedom of association" would be difficult to reconcile with Vietnam's single, state-sponsored labor union. Producers in several industries worry that the TPP's environmental provisions could raise costs. As the country with the lowest per capita income in the TPP, Vietnam hopes for "special and differential treatment," but the TPP is unlikely to include such provisions. Vietnam is projected to gain the most from the TPP and has shown flexibility on difficult issues. Much will depend on whether provisions affecting its critical textile and apparel exports are favorable enough to justify hard concessions.

Canada's TPP debate has been dominated by "supply management" in the dairy and poultry industries and by intellectual property protection. Canada imposes quotas on dairy and poultry, with tariff equivalents estimated to run to 250 percent for dairy products. Since this issue is important to New Zealand—and likely to require concessions also by the United States—resolving it could become a prerequisite for a successful TPP outcome. With respect to intellectual property, Canada recently passed a complex copyright bill updating its intel-

(continued on next page)

lectual property system. However, the bill is not fully consistent with proposals reportedly tabled in the TPP negotiations by Australia and the United States. These issues generate limited but forceful opposition in Canada, complicated by the diverging interests of Canada's provinces.

Japan is probably the country with the most difficult road ahead, should it join the TPP negotiations. The most important concern is agriculture: Protection levels are high, and Japan's powerful agricultural cooperatives have organized a massive campaign against the TPP. The farm lobby has been joined by the Japan Medical Association, which is concerned that services sector liberalization would erode its influence over the government-run health system by permitting private provision of health services and insurance. The government also faces difficult decisions on establishing a level playing field in financial markets served by its postal savings system. Although the TPP and other trade agreements are strongly supported by business, Japan's fragile politics and other policy challenges have made it impossible for the government to move forward on the TPP so far.

In sum, there is already spirited opposition to the TPP in most participating countries, reflecting various combinations of special business lobbies and public interest groups. These negative views also dominate online commentary on the negotiations. Significant educational initiatives and political effort will be required to build support for an agreement, regardless of its estimated benefits.

Asia-Pacific region and beyond. This would have been an ambitious strategy even when the United States played a truly dominant role in world trade, but it now has to be deployed in the midst of much uncertainty and the fragmentation of economic influence among several trading powers, including China.

The results of this study suggest that investing effort in the TPP, despite the inauspicious circumstances, is in the interest of the United States and its partner economies. If economic interests matter, the strategy should be successful in establishing a beachhead of high-quality rules. And if this template generates the gains that this study envisions, the integration effort would gain momentum and attract additional partners.

We project that US income gains under the TPP would reach $59 billion per year by 2020 and would continue to grow thereafter, although more slowly, to $78 billion per year by 2025 (figure 6.1, black dashed line). If the track then leads to an FTAAP based on the TPP template, US benefits would rise sharply to $328 billion per year in 2025 (figure 6.1, black solid line). US income would be essentially unaffected by the implementation of the Asian track. The estimated income gains are too small to register visually in the figure, but they are slightly positive, suggesting that the United States will benefit slightly from the efficiency gains that Asian integration generates. If in 2020 the Asian track continues on to the FTAAP, US benefits would rise

Figure 6.1 US income gains, 2010–25

billions of 2007 dollars

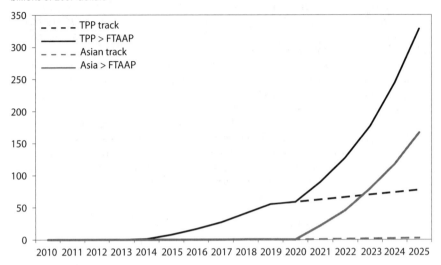

Source: Authors' estimates.

to $167 billion. And if both tracks move forward and a compromise FTAAP is adopted, US benefits would increase to $267 billion, in between the values attributed to TPP and Asian templates.

US exports would increase by $576 billion, or 21 percent relative to the 2025 baseline under the compromise FTAAP scenario (table 4.2 in chapter 4).[2] Of this increase, agriculture and mining would account for $31 billion, manufacturing for $168 billion, and services for $376 billion, the last increasing by 41 percent relative to the baseline. While reinforcing all US exports, regionwide free trade would most dramatically boost exports of sophisticated goods and services.

Given these large changes, the adjustment burdens appear to be surprisingly modest. The simulations suggest that annual job shifts on the TPP track, as defined in chapter 4, would rise to 40,000 to 50,000 jobs per year in the 2014–17 period (figure 6.2). They would rise further to roughly 100,000 jobs per year in the final two years of TPP implementation in 2018–19. For perspective, US employment levels will be in the 161 million to 165 million range in those years, and the United States will have to create 900,000 *new* jobs each year to sustain full employment. In any given year, TPP-related job shifts would affect roughly two to six workers in every 10,000 and a small fraction of

---

2. Both exports and imports would grow since the trade balance is assumed to be constant across trade initiatives. This follows standard theory in linking the current account balance to macroeconomic rather than trade policy determinants.

Figure 6.2   Adjustment to the TPP: Job shifts and income gains per job shift

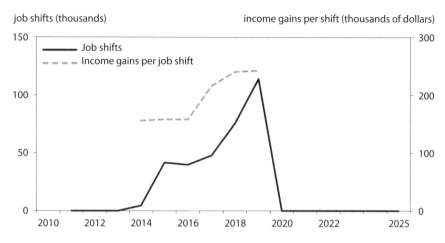

Source: Authors' estimates.

normal replacement flows in the labor force. Meanwhile, the TPP track would generate annual benefits rising from $8 billion to $59 billion. For the 2014–19 period as a whole, national income would rise by $459,000 per job shift, representing about nine years of average worker compensation for each change required. Moreover, the income gains would continue after implementation is completed and no further job shifts are required.

The FTAAP is a larger project and would impose larger adjustments. During the 2020–25 period, the implementation of the FTAAP would increase job shifts to around 300,000 annually, affecting 18 workers of every 10,000. But the average ratio of income gains to shifts would also rise, to $539,000 per job shift, covering average annual compensation more than tenfold. Once the FTAAP is fully implemented in 2025, adjustments would tail off to nearly zero, but the benefits would continue to increase with Asia-Pacific economic growth.

The results suggest that the benefits of the TPP for the United States are significant, potentially adding $300 billion per year to US incomes under some scenarios. While adjustments will be required to benefit from the agreements, the gains would be high compared with the adjustment burden—nine to ten times the compensation of an average worker for each worker who has to change jobs. An ultimate regionwide or global agreement would be especially attractive to the United States, multiplying its gains by a factor of three to four.

China

China's remarkable economic progress reflects bold decisions taken in the early 1990s to open and modernize its economy, leading to major market reforms and accession to the WTO. These decisions have put China at the center of the world's manufacturing system, combining inputs from across the Asia-Pacific region and selling them throughout the region's markets. China has also begun to play a role in the region's policy architecture by proposing a pioneering bilateral agreement with ASEAN in 2002. It followed with Trans-Pacific agreements with Chile and Peru. In 2011, China also concluded negotiations on a trilateral investment treaty with Japan and Korea and is discussing launching FTA negotiations with a number of countries in the Asia-Pacific region.

Given China's scale and strategic role in the region, it is difficult to envision the future of an Asia-Pacific trading system without a central role for China. China has yet to play that role in either the global or the regional system, and its trade policies remain fluid. It has carried out most of its WTO accession obligations and has complied with WTO dispute resolution rulings, but it has not joined the Government Procurement Agreement (as envisioned at accession) or brought its influence to bear on concluding the Doha Round negotiations. China still appears to face too many challenges at home to become a major supplier of global public goods.

Since China and the United States are unlikely to agree on the terms of a comprehensive, high-quality trade and investment agreement at this time, the TPP and Asian tracks are likely to move in parallel for now, with the United States and China competing to strengthen these tracks. China has actively promoted the China-Japan-Korea agreement in recent years, and it has shown flexibility in the design of an ASEAN-based regional agreement, agreeing to let the RCEP proposal move forward. While interdependence with the United States is high and numerous bilateral exchanges are under way, agreement on a common policy framework appears to be some time away.

Hopefully the environment for cooperation will improve. If China's economy enters a new wave of reforms, as is quite likely, its positions may change on divisive issues such as government procurement, the environment, state-owned enterprises, and even intellectual property. Similarly, if the US economy recovers and becomes more comfortable with its "pivot to Asia," it should have more appetite for initiatives that strengthen linkages with China. In the meantime, the two economies could pursue smaller, step-wise compromises to build the foundations for cooperation in the future.

The time path of China's income changes on the TPP track (figure 6.3, black dashed line) shows initial losses due to trade diversion, rising from $1 billion in 2014 to $28 billion in 2020 and $47 billion in 2025. These are the largest diversion effects calculated in the study. One part of these losses is preference erosion; China already has an FTA with most members of the TPP, which would now grant preferences similar to those available to China to the United States and other TPP partners. (Some American observers call this "leveling the playing field.") The second and more important part is trade diversion; some of China's competitors, including Vietnam, Malaysia, Mexico,

Figure 6.3 China's income gains, 2010–25

billions of 2007 dollars

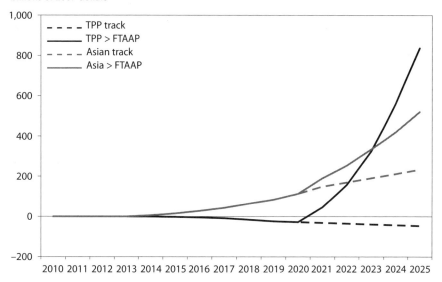

Source: Authors' estimates.

Japan, and Korea, would gain preferential access to US and other TPP markets relative to China.

China's gains on the Asian track (figure 6.3, grey dashed line) would offset some of these preferences (for example, in Japanese and Korean markets), compensating for losses from the development of the TPP. Income gains would rise from $6 billion in 2014 to $233 billion in 2025. These gains would reflect trade creation with Japan and Korea and eventually more efficient production throughout the Asian region under an ASEAN+3 agreement. The big prize would still be a comprehensive Asia-Pacific agreement, which could be reached, as we have seen, through several pathways. Chinese gains from the FTAAP would be quite large, ranging from $521 billion, or 4 percent of projected GDP, under an Asian template, to $837 billion, or 7 percent of projected GDP, under a TPP template. Although the Asian template favors China's industries and thus allows China to capture a larger share of the benefits, the TPP template leads to deeper liberalization, which dominates the absolute gains.

China has a significant stake in the Asian track and especially, given its global scale, in regionwide integration. Its benefits—as those of the United States—reach their potential only with an Asia-Pacific or wider agreement, which would increase Chinese income gains by a factor of 3.6. Indeed, our simulations suggest that China would be the largest beneficiary of the FTAAP, capturing one-third of the total gains produced by the agreement. Some

Chinese commentators have recommended that China take a positive view of both the TPP and Asian tracks and promote progress toward an inclusive regional agreement. Still, the dominant reaction in China today appears to be negative toward an integration path that involves the United States.

Japan

Potential Asia-Pacific trade agreements offer Japan large benefits, but current sluggish economic growth and political uncertainty appear to be paralyzing Japanese policymaking. Japan's labor force is expected to decline by 12 percent over the next 15 years; concerns run high about adjustment, the "hollowing out" of manufacturing, and possible unemployment. Given stable or declining markets, employment in several sectors will have to shrink. The background level of adjustment under the baseline scenario is high; around 1 percent of the labor force will need to shift jobs each year. Some employment cutbacks may involve retiring workers, but there is no necessary relationship between structural shifts and retirement patterns.

Against this background, Japan desperately needs dynamic new markets abroad, yet it is falling behind Korea and other competitors on improving its access through trade policy. Japan has an Economic Partnership Agreement (EPA) with ASEAN but not with the United States or Europe, or with China and Korea. Its business community is actively promoting trade negotiations with Asian partners and the United States.

The results of this study amply justify an active FTA policy. Both the TPP and Asian tracks generate substantial and roughly equal income gains for Japan in the neighborhood of 2 percent of GDP (figure 6.4, dashed lines). The benefits under the TPP would be derived to a large extent from inward investment and improvements in services productivity, and under the Asian agreement from goods trade, with exports increasing by 18 percent. Unlike China and the United States, Japan can potentially join both integration tracks and hence achieve substantial access to virtually all regional markets even without a regionwide agreement. The implementation of both tracks would increase Japanese incomes by nearly 4 percent of GDP. Full implementation of the FTAAP would offer only modest additional benefits, raising incomes instead by an additional 0.4 percent of GDP.

Yet both tracks face strong political opposition. In the case of the TPP, the opposition is energized by potential concessions in agriculture and other areas of economic governance, such as access to insurance and other services sectors and changes in the postal savings system. Potential membership has attracted particularly vocal political opposition. In the case of the Asian track, economic concerns are less prominent since it is expected that Japan will be able to exclude politically sensitive sectors. But there is strong concern about political relations with China, which have become more tense in recent years. Meanwhile, Japan's political tensions make it difficult to take controversial decisions, no matter how beneficial they may be in the long run.

Figure 6.4 Japan's income gains, 2010–25

billions of 2007 dollars

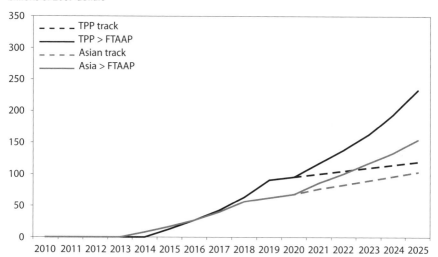

Source: Authors' estimates.

Japan would benefit from both the Asian and TPP tracks and the case for aggressive Japanese commercial policy is compelling. However, Japan's difficult political environment highlights the challenge of liberalization in the context of a declining labor force. Such an economy faces a high "background" adjustment burden due to slow demand and multiple declining sectors. This inevitable adjustment makes it difficult for governments to adopt policies that would require still faster adjustment, even if those policies offer the best prospects for reaching dynamic new markets. The lesson for countries that will face similar constraints in the future is to act early—it becomes increasingly difficult to make decisions that require adjustment once growth rates decline.

Other Economies

The simulations provide results for 24 world regions and produce far too much detailed information to be discussed in this Policy Analysis. The following five cases give a flavor of findings for countries other than the three discussed so far; they are far from exhaustive but illustrate important common patterns.

Vietnam would be the largest beneficiary on the TPP track and of an Asia-Pacific-wide agreement. Five factors explain this result: strong trade with the United States; high protection abroad against apparel and footwear, which are Vietnam's principal exports; strong competitive positions in these and other manufacturing industries where China's comparative advantage is fading; high initial domestic protection; and powerful scale effects in Vietnam's principal production clusters. The first three factors boost Vietnamese exports and terms of trade under the TPP. The last two amplify these benefits by stimulating productivity gains. Higher incomes in turn enable Vietnam to invest more and grow more rapidly. Of course, Vietnam would face significant challenges in implementing an agreement that requires stringent disciplines in areas such as labor and government procurement. It also faces tough challenges in maintaining a macroeconomic environment that permits adjustment and encourages long-term investments. But overall, Vietnam's participation in the agreement is well founded.

Korea would gain significantly from all tracks due to the importance of trade in its economy. Korea has been aggressive in pursuing integration opportunities and will most likely access both the TPP and Asian tracks. Since much of its trade—including with the United States and the European Union—is already covered by FTAs, the main source of additional gains now depends on access to Chinese and Japanese markets. The Asian track provides a route to this goal, generating income gains of $87 billion by 2025 (table 4.1 in chapter 4). With that agreement, Korea would have essentially free trade with all Asia-Pacific partners. Korean policymakers have accordingly signaled that the China-Japan-Korea agreement is Korea's next priority, although they remain interested in eventually joining the TPP because it would provide more effective rules for Korea's emerging high-technology industries. If the China-Japan-Korea agreement did not materialize, Korea could complete a bilateral agreement with China and obtain the benefits from Japan-Korea liberalization through the TPP. Through its trade diplomacy, Korea has moved ahead of most advanced countries in completing or at least launching the adjustments required by the changing global environment. Assuming Korea pursues both the TPP and Asian tracks, it will achieve 89 percent of the benefits of regionwide integration and is likely, at that point, to shift its sights to global or extraregional opportunities.

Thailand is not assumed to participate in the TPP track at this time but would see large benefits from the FTAAP, estimated at 5 percent of GDP (table 4.1). A special scenario, not reported in this study, also suggests large benefits for Thailand from joining the TPP, similar to those of Malaysia and much larger than the benefits it can obtain on the Asian track. New trade agreements would improve Thai productivity and increase exports of vehicles and electrical equipment. Like Vietnam, Thailand could make headway in building industrial clusters, including in industries that become contested as Chinese wages rise. All this suggests that if the TPP track gains momentum, and if Thailand's internal politics are stable enough to make negotiations viable, Thailand can be expected to join the TPP. Otherwise Thailand's position will be similar to that of China; short of a regionwide agreement, the TPP would put Thailand at a disadvantage compared with competitors with preferential access to US markets. Unlike China, it is relatively free to pursue negotiations on both tracks.

Russia was not assumed to be part of either track, but as a member of APEC it would be a candidate for the FTAAP. Until such an agreement is reached (2020 in our scenarios), Russia would suffer slight trade diversion, leading to losses of around 0.1 percent of GDP. But if Russia does gain access to the FTAAP as an APEC member, its income gains would be 9 percent of GDP, one of the largest of all participants. Its exports would rise by 28 percent relative to baseline. In effect, the FTAAP would offer Russia entry into Trans-Pacific markets, as well as impose policy changes that would boost Russian competitiveness. Of course, many changes—including broad services and investment liberalization—would be required, and Russia may not be ready politically to accept such reforms. But if Russia is committed to opening its markets and building regional ties, it could emerge as the surprise champion of regionwide integration.

India was not assumed to participate in this study's main liberalization scenarios, but there are good reasons to expect that its linkages with the Asia-Pacific region will intensify. Since India competes with Asian economies in some of its production, it was projected to experience trade diversion losses of around 0.6 percent of GDP in the case of the FTAAP. More importantly, India would miss out on the domestic productivity benefits associated with liberalization and regional integration. However, deregulation and "look East" policies could put India within reach of fuller integration in the Asia-Pacific economy. These efforts could lead to regional agreements such as the RCEP, or membership in APEC and eventual regionwide negotiations. But more reforms will be needed before India's domestic policies become compatible with the expectations of the TPP or even Asian tracks. In any case, we examined adding India to the FTAAP in a special simulation and projected large gains of 6 percent of GDP for India in 2025. Moreover, adding India increased the benefits realized by nearly all other countries, by as much as one-third in the case of Singapore. Other significant winners from Indian membership would include Australia, Canada, Chile, and Malaysia. Asian economies were also found to gain, but less, since they would face more direct Indian competition.

The fine-grained results point out that all countries in the region will be affected by, and will have to respond to, the evolving TPP and Asian agreements. The details suggest potential new champions for each of the tracks and possibly striking policy changes in some countries as the tracks gather momentum. In a sense, TPP and Asian integration will jolt the equilibrium of economic relationships; their competitive consequences could include widespread competitive liberalization as well as domestic reform. The challenge lies in harnessing these energies in tracks that converge on regionwide, and perhaps global, free trade.

7

Conclusion

The potential economic effects of the TPP and Asian trade agreements are significant, competitive, and complementary. We found that each track could generate substantial, widely distributed gains for members as well as incentives for enlargement. The potential endpoint of the tracks—a regionwide agreement such as the FTAAP—could generate nearly $1.3 trillion to $2.4 trillion in global benefits, much more than those expected from a successful Doha Round.

Four key implications emerge. First, the benefits are likely to be substantial on both tracks for all members. The early stages of the tracks would favor smaller, low-income economies such as Vietnam; the middle stages larger countries like Japan and Korea; and the final stages China and the United States. Gains would be derived primarily from trade and investment creation and not from trade diversion from excluded economies; larger Asia-Pacific country groups are "natural" trading blocs based on efficient specialization.

Second, the templates used matter; they significantly affect the gains from integration. The template emerging on the TPP track is expected to be more comprehensive, with rigorous disciplines also in sectors important to advanced countries, such as services, investment, and intellectual property. The template emerging on the Asian track is more likely to focus on the manufacturing production chains of Asian economies, and it may have numerous exceptions for sensitive sectors and regulations. Since the TPP template implies deeper liberalization, it would generate greater benefits, including for China and other Asian economies if the template is adopted regionwide. The tracks define "disagreement points" in the effort to shape the ultimate rules of Asia-Pacific economic relations.

Third, adjustment burdens appear to be modest compared with benefits, even in the short run when economies experience the greatest transitional impacts from integration. (Adjustment burdens were estimated empirically as the sum of intersectoral job shifts.) In the peak adjustment period in the United States, for example, the TPP and FTAAP produce benefits equivalent to 8 to 10 years of compensation for each job shifted from one sector to another.

Fourth, the tracks are likely to follow a dynamic that leads to regionwide integration. Initially, the economies of China and the United States will be magnets for expanding trade agreements, attracting smaller economies to each track and generating competition between them for members. As larger economies such as Japan and Korea join the tracks, the value of membership will grow, further stimulating enlargement on both tracks. In the end, many Asia-Pacific economies are likely to be members of both tracks, with preferential access to virtually all regional markets. That would leave China and the United States among the relatively few countries *without* regionwide preferential access, giving them strong incentive to promote the consolidation of the tracks.

That eventual consolidation of the tracks, say a decade or so from now, should generate greater gains at lower costs for China and the United States than such an agreement would today. Much will still depend on their political relationship, but the growth of China-US bilateral trade and investment, especially if supported by a decade of cooperation, economic progress and reform in China, and the reinvigoration of the US economy, could greatly improve the environment for formal agreements. The opportunities for further integration would then also attract interest from Europe and other major trading partners and could lead to the resumption of global negotiations. This is a highly speculative scenario, and much could go wrong with it, but the gains associated with its results justify vigorous study and political support.

This study has presented an assessment of the TPP and Asian tracks from a methodological and technical perspective, without translating the findings into detailed policy recommendations. We do think that important policy implications emerge, but recommendations will have to be based on more detailed analyses of the interests and political environment of specific countries. A separate paper by two of us (Petri and Plummer 2012) has examined policy implications for the United States. Broadly, it recommends that the United States (1) pursue an early conclusion to the current TPP negotiations, (2) strive for high standards in the TPP but without jeopardizing the prospects for a regionwide agreement, (3) attempt to establish a dialogue between the TPP and Asian tracks to encourage consistency between them, and (4) intensify its engagement with China on a "third track" of discussions to create building blocks for future regional free trade. We believe that similar policy conclusions could also emerge for other countries based on the evidence provided by this study. The study builds on a long modeling tradition and introduces innovations in methodology and data. But its estimates are hardly free from error. Nor can they capture the many intangible effects of major policy initiatives. Large, new trade agreements in the Asia-Pacific could lend momentum to global economic integration. Similar waves of economic integration appear to have contributed to the acceleration of world economic growth in the past and have encouraged the convergence of policies toward pragmatic market-based models.

The Trans-Pacific and Asian integration tracks are ambitious, positive-sum projects that promise substantial benefits and could lead to Asia-Pacific free trade and, more generally, to a more peaceful and prosperous world economy. Of course, the geopolitical environment may not support this trajectory. Economics is not the whole story, but it matters and strongly favors the Asia-Pacific initiatives examined in this study.

Appendices

Appendix A
The Computable General Equilibrium Model

Data and Dimensions

The model is based on the preliminary GTAP8 dataset for 2007. It consists of 24 regions and 18 sectors (table A.1).

Production and Trade

Agriculture, mining, and government services sectors are assumed to exhibit perfect competition. In each of these sectors, a representative firm operates under constant returns to scale technology. Trade is modeled using the Armington assumption for import demand. Manufacturing and private services are characterized by monopolistic competition, and their structure of production and trade follows Melitz (2003). Each sector with monopolistic competition consists of a continuum of firms that are differentiated by the varieties they produce and their productivity. Firms face fixed production costs, resulting in increasing returns to scale. Fixed and variable costs are also associated with exporting activities.

On the demand side, agents have Dixit-Stiglitz preferences over the continuum of varieties. As each firm is a monopolist for the variety it produces, it sets the price of its product at a constant markup over marginal cost. A firm enters domestic or export markets if and only if the net profit generated from such sales is sufficient to cover fixed costs. This zero-cutoff profit condition defines the productivity thresholds for firms entering domestic and exports markets and in turn determines the equilibrium distribution of nonexporting and exporting firms as well as their average productivities. Usually, the combi-

Table A.1 Model regions and sectors

	Region		Sector
1	Australia	1	Rice
2	New Zealand	2	Wheat
3	China	3	Other agriculture
4	Hong Kong	4	Mining
5	Japan	5	Food and beverages
6	Korea	6	Textiles
7	Taiwan	7	Apparel and footwear
8	Indonesia	8	Chemicals
9	Malaysia	9	Metals
10	Philippines	10	Electrical equipment
11	Singapore	11	Machinery
12	Thailand	12	Transportation equipment
13	Vietnam	13	Other manufactures
14	Brunei Darussalam	14	Utilities
15	India	15	Construction
16	Canada	16	Trade, transportation, and communications
17	United States	17	Private services
18	Mexico	18	Government services
19	Chile		
20	Peru		
21	Russia		
22	Europe[a]		
23	Other ASEAN[b]		
24	Rest of world		

a. European Union 25, Iceland, and Switzerland.
b. Cambodia, Lao PDR, and Myanmar.

Source: Authors' specification.

nation of a fixed export cost and a variable (iceberg) export cost ensures that the exporting productivity threshold is higher than that for production for the domestic market, so that only a fraction of firms with high productivity export. These firms supply both domestic and export markets. The number of firms in the monopolistic sectors is assumed to be fixed.

Production technology in each sector is modeled using nested constant elasticity of substitution (CES) functions. At the top level, the output is produced as a combination of aggregate intermediate demand and value added. At the second level, aggregate intermediate demand is split into each commodity according to Leontief technology. Value added is produced by a capital-land bundle and aggregate labor. Finally, at the bottom level, aggregate labor is decomposed into unskilled and skilled labor, and the capital-land bundle is decomposed into capital and land (for the agricultural sector) or natural resources (for the mining sector). At each level of production, a unit cost function is dual to the CES aggregator function and demand functions for corresponding inputs. The top-level unit cost function defines the marginal cost of sectoral output.

Income Distribution, Demand, and Factor Markets

Incomes generated from production accrue to a single representative household in each region. A household maximizes utility using the Extended Linear Expenditure System, which is derived from maximizing the Stone-Geary utility function. The consumption/saving decision is completely static. Saving enter the utility function as a "good" and its price is set as equal to the average price of consumer goods. Investment demand and government consumption are specified as a Leontief function. In each sector a composite good defined by the Dixit-Stiglitz aggregator over domestic and imported varieties is used for final and intermediate demand.

All commodity and factor markets are assumed to clear through price adjustment. There are five primary factors of production. Capital, agricultural land, and two types of labor (skilled and unskilled) are fully mobile across sectors within a region. In forestry, fishing, and mining, a sector-specific factor is introduced into the production function to reflect resource constraints. For all primary factors, stocks are fixed.

Macro Closure

There are three macro closures in the model: the net government balance, the trade balance, and the investment and savings balance. We assume that government consumption and saving are exogenous in real terms. Any changes in the government budget are automatically compensated by changes in income tax rates on households.

The second closure concerns the current account balance. In each region, foreign savings are set exogenously. With the price index of OECD manufacturing exports being chosen as the numéraire of the model, equilibrium on the foreign account is achieved by changing the relative prices across regions, which can be interpreted as changing real exchange rates.

Domestic investment is the endogenous sum of household savings, government savings, and foreign savings. As government and foreign savings are exogenous, changes in investment are determined by changes in the levels of household saving. This closure rule corresponds to the "neoclassical" macroeconomic closure in the CGE literature.

Appendix B
Baseline Projections

Table B.1 Baseline GDP projections

Economy	GDP (billions of 2007 dollars)				Growth rate, 2010–25 (percent)	Share of world (percent)	
	2010	2015	2020	2025		2010	2025
TPP track economies	17,860	20,587	23,399	26,502	2.7	30.6	25.7
United States	14,050	16,021	18,057	20,273	2.5	24.0	19.6
Australia	922	1,080	1,248	1,433	3.0	1.6	1.4
Canada	1,425	1,617	1,794	1,978	2.2	2.4	1.9
Chile	162	201	243	292	4.0	0.3	0.3
Mexico	1,031	1,326	1,635	2,004	4.5	1.8	1.9
New Zealand	137	158	178	201	2.6	0.2	0.2
Peru	132	184	244	320	6.1	0.2	0.3
Asian track economies	6,047	9,537	14,358	20,084	8.3	10.3	19.5
China	4,850	7,948	12,226	17,249	8.8	8.3	16.7
Hong Kong	217	268	332	406	4.3	0.4	0.4
Indonesia	550	784	1,114	1,549	7.1	0.9	1.5
Philippines	163	200	252	322	4.6	0.3	0.3
Thailand	266	336	434	558	5.1	0.5	0.5
Two-track economies	5,902	6,739	7,664	8,660	2.6	10.1	8.4
Brunei	13	15	18	20	2.9	0	0
Japan	4,250	4,635	5,006	5,338	1.5	7.3	5.2
Korea	1,135	1,406	1,734	2,117	4.2	1.9	2.1

Malaysia	207	270	343	431	5.0	0.4	0.4
Singapore	202	267	337	415	4.9	0.3	0.4
Vietnam	94	146	227	340	8.9	0.2	0.3
Other	28,636	34,192	40,531	47,977	3.5	49.0	46.5
Russia	1,358	1,757	2,256	2,865	5.1	2.3	2.8
Taiwan	420	539	682	840	4.7	0.7	0.8
Europe	16,629	18,743	20,719	22,714	2.1	28.5	22.0
India	1,559	2,405	3,614	5,233	8.4	2.7	5.1
Other ASEAN	34	45	61	83	6.2	0.1	0.1
Rest of world	8,637	10,703	13,200	16,241	4.3	14.8	15.7
World	58,445	71,056	85,952	103,223	3.9	100.0	100.0
Memorandum							
TPP	23,762	27,326	31,063	35,162	2.6	40.7	34.1
ASEAN+3	11,982	16,322	22,083	28,828	6.0	20.5	27.9
APEC	31,587	39,160	48,358	58,951	4.2	54.0	57.1

Source: Authors' estimates.

Table B.2   Baseline export projections

Economy	Exports (billions of 2007 dollars)				Growth rate, 2010–25 (percent)	Share of world (percent)	
	2010	2015	2020	2025		2010	2025
TPP track economies	2,532	3,169	3,813	4,555	4.0	17.4	16
United States	1,536	1,927	2,341	2,813	4.1	10.6	9.9
Australia	176	226	275	332	4.3	1.2	1.2
Canada	418	469	530	597	2.4	2.9	2.1
Chile	69	94	120	151	5.4	0.5	0.5
Mexico	266	353	422	507	4.4	1.8	1.8
New Zealand	34	44	52	60	4.0	0.2	0.2
Peru	35	57	74	95	6.9	0.2	0.3
Asian track economies	2,206	3,234	4,455	5,971	6.9	15.2	21.0
China	1,622	2,366	3,363	4,597	7.2	11.2	16.2
Hong Kong	132	173	203	235	3.9	0.9	0.8
Indonesia	172	276	373	501	7.4	1.2	1.8
Philippines	77	122	140	163	5.2	0.5	0.6
Thailand	203	297	377	476	5.9	1.4	1.7
Two-track economies	1,691	2,209	2,512	2,817	3.5	11.6	9.9
Brunei	4	5	7	9	5.6	0	0
Japan	833	1,004	1,128	1,252	2.8	5.7	4.4
Korea	386	581	658	718	4.2	2.7	2.5

Malaysia	189	260	295	336	3.9	1.3	1.2
Singapore	210	246	256	263	1.5	1.4	0.9
Vietnam	70	113	168	239	8.5	0.5	0.8
Other	8,091	11,040	12,853	15,072	4.2	55.7	53.0
Russia	359	581	796	1,071	7.6	2.5	3.8
Taiwan	281	453	574	712	6.4	1.9	2.5
Europe	4,753	6,472	6,947	7,431	3.0	32.7	26.2
India	207	333	539	869	10.1	1.4	3.1
Other ASEAN	12	19	25	34	7.3	0.1	0.1
Rest of world	2,480	3,182	3,972	4,955	4.7	17.1	17.4
World	14,520	19,653	23,633	28,415	4.6	100.0	100.0
Memorandum							
TPP	4,223	5,379	6,325	7,372	3.8	29.1	25.9
ASEAN+3	3,909	5,462	6,993	8,822	5.6	26.9	31.0
APEC	7,069	9,647	12,150	15,126	5.2	48.7	53.2

Source: Authors' estimates.

Table B.3 Baseline import projections

Economy	Imports (billions of 2007 dollars)				Growth rate, 2010–25 (percent)	Share of world (percent)	
	2010	2015	2020	2025		2010	2025
TPP track economies	3,293	3,963	4,643	5,430	3.4	21.8	18.3
United States	2,209	2,626	3,069	3,577	3.3	14.6	12.0
Australia	201	252	303	361	4.0	1.3	1.2
Canada	464	519	583	655	2.3	3.1	2.2
Chile	72	100	127	161	5.5	0.5	0.5
Mexico	271	357	426	511	4.3	1.8	1.7
New Zealand	40	50	59	69	3.8	0.3	0.2
Peru	35	57	74	96	6.9	0.2	0.3
Asian track economies	1,906	2,933	4,143	5,647	7.5	12.6	19.0
China	1,332	2,066	3,042	4,253	8.0	8.8	14.3
Hong Kong	135	186	226	269	4.7	0.9	0.9
Indonesia	161	263	358	483	7.6	1.1	1.6
Philippines	88	132	151	175	4.7	0.6	0.6
Thailand	191	286	367	468	6.1	1.3	1.6
Two-track economies	1,578	2,150	2,505	2,874	4.1	10.4	9.7
Brunei	3	5	7	9	6.3	0	0
Japan	738	934	1,084	1,238	3.5	4.9	4.2
Korea	403	616	711	792	4.6	2.7	2.7

Malaysia	162	235	271	315	4.5	1.1	1.1
Singapore	194	240	261	281	2.5	1.3	0.9
Vietnam	77	119	172	240	7.9	0.5	0.8
Other	8,334	11,418	13,381	15,782	4.3	55.2	53.1
Russia	300	510	718	986	8.3	2.0	3.3
Taiwan	245	419	542	684	7.1	1.6	2.3
Europe	5,039	6,868	7,463	8,094	3.2	33.3	27.2
India	267	392	594	916	8.6	1.8	3.1
Other ASEAN	15	22	29	37	6.4	0.1	0.1
Rest of world	2,469	3,206	4,035	5,067	4.9	16.3	17.0
World	15,112	20,463	24,672	29,734	4.6	100.0	100.0
Memorandum							
TPP	4,871	6,112	7,148	8,304	3.6	32.2	27.9
ASEAN+3	3,499	5,105	6,677	8,558	6.1	23.2	28.8
APEC	7,322	9,975	12,551	15,620	5.2	48.5	52.5

Source: Authors' estimates.

Table B.4 Baseline outward FDI stock projections

Economy	Outward FDI stocks (billions of 2007 dollars)				Growth rate, 2010–25 (perent)	Share of world (percent)	
	2010	2015	2020	2025		2010	2025
TPP track economies	4,360	6,005	8,140	10,980	6.4	20.6	20.8
United States	3,474	4,770	6,461	8,705	6.3	16.4	16.5
Australia	239	339	475	660	7.0	1.1	1.2
Canada	567	772	1,020	1,343	5.9	2.7	2.5
Chile	10	16	25	39	9.5	0	0.1
Mexico	59	91	134	199	8.5	0.3	0.4
New Zealand	11	15	21	29	7.0	0.1	0.1
Peru	1	2	4	7	11.3	0	0
Asian track economies	775	1,403	2,495	4,247	12.0	3.7	8.0
China	261	536	1,039	1,859	14.0	1.2	3.5
Hong Kong	479	801	1,336	2,171	10.6	2.3	4.1
Indonesia	5	11	23	44	14.9	0	0.1
Philippines	6	11	18	30	11.1	0	0.1
Thailand	24	43	80	143	12.7	0.1	0.3
Two-track economies	1,342	2,018	3,038	4,529	8.4	6.3	8.6
Brunei	3	7	12	22	13.4	0	0
Japan	861	1,187	1,622	2,172	6.4	4.1	4.1
Korea	129	219	368	607	10.9	0.6	1.1

Malaysia	76	132	228	388	11.5	0.4	0.7
Singapore	272	472	806	1,336	11.2	1.3	2.5
Vietnam	1	1	2	4	13.3	0	0
Other	14,674	19,303	25,309	33,055	5.6	69.4	62.6
Russia	254	378	582	883	8.7	1.2	1.7
Taiwan	56	103	189	330	12.5	0.3	0.6
Europe	13,365	17,215	21,960	27,737	5.0	63.2	52.5
India	49	92	168	298	12.8	0.2	0.6
Other ASEAN	1	1	3	5	13.8	0	0
Rest of world	949	1,513	2,406	3,802	9.7	4.5	7.2
World	21,151	28,730	38,983	52,812	6.3	100.0	100.0
Memorandum							
TPP	5,703	8,024	11,178	15,510	6.9	27.0	29.4
ASEAN+3	2,117	3,423	5,537	8,782	9.9	10.0	16.6
APEC	6,787	9,908	14,445	20,969	7.8	32.1	39.7

Source: Authors' estimates.

Table B.5 Baseline inward FDI stock projections

| Economy | Inward FDI stocks (billions of 2007 dollars) | | | | Growth rate 2010–25 (percent) | Share of world (percent) | |
	2010	2015	2020	2025		2010	2025
TPP track economies	3,794	5,048	6,571	8,507	5.5	17.9	16.1
United States	2,375	3,080	3,912	4,929	5.0	11.2	9.3
Australia	396	550	751	1,017	6.5	1.9	1.9
Canada	571	756	971	1,239	5.3	2.7	2.3
Chile	129	193	283	416	8.1	0.6	0.8
Mexico	233	342	476	660	7.2	1.1	1.2
New Zealand	65	89	118	156	6.0	0.3	0.3
Peru	24	38	59	91	9.4	0.1	0.2
Asian track economies	1,793	3,295	5,868	9,882	12.1	8.5	18.7
China	1,045	2,042	3,770	6,443	12.9	4.9	12.2
Hong Kong	453	775	1,315	2,161	11.0	2.1	4.1
Indonesia	140	243	423	725	11.6	0.7	1.4
Philippines	28	40	57	83	7.6	0.1	0.2
Thailand	127	194	303	472	9.1	0.6	0.9
Two-track economies	923	1,344	1,938	2,784	7.6	4.4	5.3
Brunei	1	1	2	2	6.4	0	0
Japan	243	307	382	466	4.4	1.1	0.9
Korea	117	167	235	329	7.1	0.6	0.6

Malaysia	85	132	202	307	8.9	0.4	0.6
Singapore	456	699	1,052	1,564	8.6	2.2	3.0
Vietnam	22	38	67	116	11.8	0.1	0.2
Other	14,641	19,043	24,605	31,639	5.3	69.2	59.9
Russia	386	557	826	1,205	7.9	1.8	2.3
Taiwan	50	74	108	155	7.9	0.2	0.3
Europe	11,959	15,080	18,768	23,077	4.5	56.5	43.7
India	173	313	551	943	12.0	0.8	1.8
Other ASEAN	12	20	34	60	11.5	0.1	0.1
Rest of world	2,060	2,999	4,319	6,199	7.6	9.7	11.7
World	21,151	28,730	38,983	52,812	6.3	100.0	100.0
Memorandum							
TPP	4,717	6,392	8,509	11,291	6.0	22.3	21.4
ASEAN+3	2,728	4,659	7,841	12,726	10.8	12.9	24.1
APEC	6,946	10,318	15,311	22,533	8.2	32.8	42.7

Source: Authors' estimates.

Appendix C
Scoring Provisions in Asia-Pacific Agreements

Trade agreements contain detailed provisions and are difficult to summarize. Nevertheless, efforts have been made in recent years to translate the content of agreements into quantitative scores that measure the strength of the agreement in distinct issue areas. Important examples of such studies are included in Findlay and Urata (2010). So far, these efforts have mainly focused on subjective judgments made by experts who assess the quality of agreements in particular areas.

This study develops new, objective measures of the content of Asia-Pacific trade agreements in 21 issue areas. The measures are based on two new datasets that provide unusually detailed information on the text of regional trade agreements. The first is a dataset derived from an inventory of 42 Asia-Pacific trade agreements compiled by APEC in 2010. This initiative collected the full text of agreements in machine-readable form and then subdivided each text into some 1,439 provisions that appeared in one or more agreements (these categories and the allocations were based on expert judgment). The resulting matrix of provisions by agreement is available online.[1] The second new dataset is provided by a WTO (2011) review of regional and bilateral trade agreements. That study examined the treatment of 21 broad issues (similar, but not identical to the issues examined in this study) in 131 different regional and bilateral agreements, including most of those covered by the APEC dataset. The WTO determined whether an agreement covered a particular issue and, if so, whether its provisions were enforceable.

---

1. The data are located at http://fta.apec.org/search.aspx. We used data accessed on August 25, 2011.

We use these sources of information to "score" how specific agreements treated 21 major issues. We first established a correspondence mapping of the issues across the two sources. We then used APEC data to calculate raw measures of the "scope" and "depth" of coverage of each issue area, and WTO data to calculate raw measures of the "enforceability" of the coverage. These measures are defined as follows:

- *Scope* of coverage is measured by calculating the share of possible provisions in an issue area that were mentioned in an agreement. For example, the APEC source lists 74 possible provisions in the "government procurement" area and NAFTA mentioned 41 of these, so the raw scope of coverage measure for this issue is 0.55.

- *Depth* of coverage is measured by counting the number of characters used in the text devoted to the issue area in an agreement.

- *Enforceability* of coverage is measured using the WTO Preferential Trade Agreement database.[2] The measure is set to 0 if the WTO found that the issue was not covered, 1 if it was covered but without enforceable provisions, and 2 if it was covered with enforceable provisions.

The three measures are transformed into standardized scores using the formula:

$$s_{ij}^{k*} = a + (1 - a)(s_{ij}^{k} - s_{i,10\%}^{k})/(s_{i,90\%}^{k} - s_{i,10\%}^{k}), \text{ such that } a < s_{ij}^{k*} < 1, \tag{C.1}$$

where s_{ij}^{k} is the kth measure for country i in issue area j, and the asterisk denotes the transformed value. Thus, the standardized measure takes the value a (arbitrarily set to 0.5) if the agreement has minimal provisions for an area (at or below the 10th percentile of agreements that mention the area) and the value 1 if the agreement has maximal provisions (at or above the 90th percentile of agreements). In between, the transformation locates each measure on the a to 1 scale based on its position in the range defined by the 10th and 90th percentiles of agreements. For example, a measure of 0.95 for "government procurement scope" means that the share of the possible provisions relating to government procurement that are addressed in an agreement falls just shy of the 90th percentile of all agreements that cover government procurement.

Finally, the three standardized measures are combined into a single score with equal weights:

$$S_{ij} = \frac{1}{3} \sum_{k} s_{ij}^{k*} \tag{C.2}$$

Unlike other scoring methodologies, this approach uses mostly objective information derived from the underlying agreements. But like other methodologies, it also rests on arbitrary assumptions. For example, it could be reason-

---

2. The data are located at http://ptadb.wto.org/?lang=1. We used data accessed on September 12, 2011.

Table C.1 Scores of provisions in Asia-Pacific agreements

	Issue	Pre-2000	2000–2005	Post-2005
1	Tariffs	0.35	0.24	0.26
2	Nontariff measures	0.40	0.28	0.50
3	E-commerce	0.53	0.64	0.71
4	State-owned enterprises	0.53	0.57	0.60
5	Agriculture	0.40	0.52	0.63
6	Rules of origin	0.48	0.63	0.72
7	Customs procedures	0.68	0.57	0.75
8	Sanitary and phytosanitary measures	0.54	0.69	0.61
9	Technical barriers to trade	0.62	0.75	0.72
10	Trade remedies	0.59	0.78	0.79
11	Government procurement	0.48	0.57	0.53
12	Investment barriers	0.49	0.62	0.74
13	Services	0.16	0.34	0.29
14	Competition	0.37	0.47	0.38
15	Intellectual property rights	0.50	0.46	0.47
16	Labor	0.39	0.23	0.13
17	Environment	0.70	0.72	0.83
18	Dispute resolution	0.55	0.55	0.63
19	Cooperation	0.00	0.09	0.34
20	Small and medium enterprises	0.00	0.01	0.12
21	Science and technology	0.05	0.19	0.41
	Average	0.42	0.47	0.53

Source: Authors' estimates.

ably argued that the several provisions used to calculate the "scope" measure are not equally important; that the words used to calculate the "depth" measure are not equally substantial; and that "enforceability" does not mean the same thing in agreements that differ in institutions and penalties. There is also no strong case for the transformation assumptions used to combine different measures into a single index. We expect, however, that the errors implied by these assumptions will partially cancel due to the unusually fine detail of the underlying information. For example, on average 70 provisions are identified in the APEC database within each issue area.

Summary scores for the 21 issue areas for agreements grouped by when they were signed are presented in table C.1. This table shows that agreements have become more rigorous over time, with average scores rising from 0.42 in pre-2000 agreements to 0.53 in post-2005 agreements. It shows considerable variation among agreements on specific provisions; for example, while traditional provisions on tariffs and nontariff measures and customs procedures vary largely randomly, there have been marked increases in scores addressing e-commerce and investment. More work will be needed to test the validity of these new results. An obvious test is whether the scores meet the "common sense" test about the rigor and scope of provisions in specific agreements. Another test is whether the scores reflect priorities that negotiators attempted to build into agreements. Still other tests could be based on the relationship of the scores to likely theoretical determinants and actual effects.

Appendix D
Quantifying the Trade Effects of Agreements

We estimate the trade effects of 57 agreements, consisting of 47 agreements already concluded but not necessarily fully implemented and 10 prospective agreements. Existing agreements are listed in table 2.1 in chapter 2, and prospective agreements in table 3.2 in chapter 3. The effects of each agreement are simulated by adjusting annual baseline values of the following sets of parameters:

- tariffs,
- utilization rates of tariff preferences,
- nontariff barriers,
- costs associated with meeting rules of origin, and
- barriers to foreign investment.

The first four sets of parameter changes are discussed below and the fifth set—affecting foreign direct investment—is discussed in appendix E. Broadly, the methodology maps the scores of issues covered in the agreements (described in appendix C) into quantitative changes in model parameters using a "policy coefficient" matrix. As other aspects of the approach, the policy matrix is subjective, but the framework allows improvements to be made as new information becomes available on prospective agreements or on how they affect barriers.

Tariffs

Regional and bilateral trade agreements typically specify preferential tariff schedules in great detail, often at the Harmonized Schedule 8-digit tariff line level. But this information is typically available only in the form of legal docu-

Figure D.1 Tariff reductions in TPP and Asian templates

reduction in MFN rate (percent)

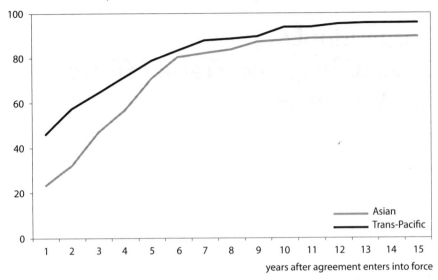

years after agreement enters into force

Source: Authors' estimates.

ments and is very difficult to use. In many cases, the schedules do not specify the base tariff rate to which the reductions will apply and they are not usually presented in a format that would facilitate machine-based access and analysis.[1] We did not have the resources to translate all of this large body of information into a usable format.

We used detailed textual information on the tariff schedules of several important agreements to develop time profiles of reduction paths over their implementation periods. For example, in analyzing such an agreement we might have determined that 40 percent of tariff lines were initially zero, 40 percent were to be reduced immediately to zero, 5 percent were to be cut by 20 percent every year over the first five years, and so on. We aggregated these tariff groups into an overall tariff reduction path for each agreement. The resulting reduction paths are shown in figure D.1. We assumed that the reduction paths for other agreements followed the paths derived from actual agreements for the same or similar countries.

In the simulations, the tariff reduction paths (such as those shown in figure D.1) were applied to base tariff rates derived from the GTAP dataset.

---

1. There are several sources of information on regional trade agreements, including WTO, ESCAP, ADB-ARIC, and APEC, but these sources generally compile the documents involved in the agreements without further analysis or standardization. An APEC effort to compile information on regional trade agreements represents a welcome step in this direction, but so far it has not resulted in a machine-accessible database.

The complication is that the GTAP data show applied tariffs, while the agreements specify reductions in MFN rates, which may be higher than applied tariffs because of reductions that are already being applied under existing bilateral or regional agreements. We therefore imputed the MFN rate from the observed applied tariff rate data taking into account information on preferential reductions that were already in effect at that time. For example, if a bilateral trade flow had an applied tariff of 15 percent in 2007 and benefited from a 25 percent preference reduction in that year (based on our analysis of regional and bilateral agreements in force), then we imputed the MFN rate to be 20 percent (15/0.75).[2]

At times more than one agreement covers trade between a pair of countries. In these cases, we assume that the tariff rate applied is the lowest of applicable rates.

Utilization of Tariff Preferences

The applied tariff rate is determined by three factors: the MFN rate, the preferential reduction available under the agreements in force, and the extent to which preferential rates are utilized. Considerable evidence indicates that FTAs are underutilized. Masahiro Kawai and Ganeshan Wignaraja (2011) find that incomplete utilization of FTAs is explained by the administrative costs of utilization, the size of the reduction offered by the agreement, and the severity of the rules of origin.

We model the utilization rate for a given agreement in terms of three elements of the agreement:

- size of the preferential tariff reduction,
- restrictiveness of the ROO, and
- size of the agreement (with larger agreements leading to higher utilization).

A score of 1 to 5 is assigned to each factor and the factors are averaged to create a composite. This score is then transformed into a utilization rate using the formula:

$$\mu = 0.8 * (s/5), \qquad\qquad (D.1)$$

where μ = utilization rate and
s = utilization score (1–5).

The rate has a maximum value of 80 percent and a minimum value of 16 percent. The values assigned to different agreements are shown in table 3.2 in chapter 3.

---

2. This example assumes that preferences are fully utilized. In practice these calculations require additional assumptions about the utilization rate of preferences as described below.

We are not aware of other studies that use such an approach to incorporate utilization rate changes into a CGE analysis of preferential agreements. One result of this approach is that the applied tariff rate may change for a bilateral trade flow even if the preferential tariff reduction is not changed, if some factor results in a higher utilization rate. For example, if an existing bilateral agreement is included in a new, larger agreement such as the TPP (or later FTAAP), the new agreement may generate higher utilization rates due to its larger size, which permits cumulation of inputs across more countries.[3] This will result in lower applied tariffs and more trade among the partners.

Nontariff Barriers

Nontariff barriers are represented in the model as "iceberg costs," that is, factors that reduce the productivity of protected activities relative to imports from efficient partners.[4] Tariff equivalents of nontariff barriers for goods are based on work by the World Bank (Kee, Nicita, and Olarreaga 2009) and Matthias Helble, Ben Shepherd, and John Wilson (2007) reported in table D.1, and for services on regressions models developed by Zhi Wang, Shashank Mohan, and Daniel Rosen (2009) (table D.2).[5] Since we completed the data preparation, the World Bank has released an additional database on services barriers; this information will need to be absorbed in a future revision of our estimates.

The estimated NTBs are assumed to represent barriers that were applied to all trade partners *prior* to any of the bilateral or regional agreements simulated in this analysis. They are reduced thereafter in amounts described below. In 2007, therefore, the NTBs that apply to a particular bilateral trade flow are assumed to be the base NTBs, reduced when appropriate by the effect of existing bilateral or regional agreements.[6]

Reductions in NTBs are calculated as a product of three factors: (1) scores of each agreement in 24 issue areas,[7] (2) policy coefficients that translate scores into reductions in different NTBs, and (3) maximum reduction rates

---

3. This assumes that each FTA allows full cumulation—e.g., the ROO count inputs from any member as originating in the FTA.

4. Some studies break the effects of NTBs into productivity losses, such as those used here, and rents. From a modeling standpoint, both approaches generate similar increases in trade, but the elimination of barriers leads to improvements in productivity only to the extent that it eliminates inefficient production rather than rents.

5. Other studies of interest include Bora, Kuwahara, and Laird (2002) and Feridhanusetyawan (2005).

6. Some analysts have suggested that a portion of NTB reductions achieved in bilateral or regional agreements, particularly in services, would generate MFN benefits and hence would also improve access for trade partners outside the agreement. That effect is not modeled in this study.

7. The list of issues was based on a composite of classifications used in the main data sources, including the APEC and WTO databases on regional trade agreements.

Table D.1   Estimated nontariff barriers on goods

Economy	World Bank Overall Trade Restrictiveness Index		Transparency index		Total index	
	Agriculture	Manufactures	Agriculture	Manufactures	Agriculture	Manufactures
Australia	0.159	0.039	0	0	0.159	0.039
Brunei[a]	0.103	0.024	0.448	0.104	0.551	0.128
Canada	0.080	0.013	0	0	0.080	0.013
Chile	0.093	0.032	0	0	0.093	0.032
China	0.102	0.051	0.232	0.116	0.334	0.167
Hong Kong	0.049	0.002	0	0	0.049	0.002
India	0.109	0.020	0.491	0.090	0.600	0.110
Indonesia	0.147	0.083	0.150	0.085	0.297	0.168
Japan	0.247	0.031	0	0	0.247	0.031
Korea[b]	0.247	0.031	0.006	0.001	0.253	0.032
Malaysia	0.349	0.149	0.106	0.045	0.455	0.194
Mexico	0.229	0.109	0.147	0.070	0.376	0.179
New Zealand	0.206	0.069	0	0	0.206	0.069
Peru	0.127	0.048	0.291	0.110	0.418	0.158
Philippines	0.343	0.152	0.409	0.181	0.752	0.333
Singapore[c]	0.049	0.002	0	0	0.049	0.002
Taiwan[b]	0.247	0.031	0	0	0.247	0.031
Thailand	0.058	0.011	0.467	0.089	0.525	0.100

(continued on next page)

Table D.1 Estimated nontariff barriers on goods *(continued)*

Economy	World Bank Overall Trade Restrictiveness Index		Transparency index		Total index	
	Agriculture	Manufactures	Agriculture	Manufactures	Agriculture	Manufactures
United States	0.110	0.037	0	0	0.110	0.037
Vietnam	0.283	0.183	0.500	0.324	0.783	0.507
Other ASEAN[d]	0.152	0.127	0.217	0.181	0.369	0.308
Russia	0.172	0.105	0.711	0.434	0.883	0.539
European Union	0.257	0.042	0	0	0.257	0.042
Rest of world[e]	0.124	0.057	0.172	0.079	0.296	0.136

a. Based on ASEAN average.
b. Based on Japan.
c. Based on Hong Kong.
d. Based on Lao PDR only.
e. Based on world average.

Sources: Kee, Nicita, and Olarreaga (2009); Helble, Shepherd, and Wilson (2007). Italics denote estimates by authors.

Table D.2   Estimated nontariff barriers on services

Economy	Utilities	Construction	Trade, transportation, and communications	Private services	Government services
Australia	0.145	0.123	0.123	0.124	0.159
Brunei	0.268	0.245	0.244	0.245	0.284
Canada	0.139	0.117	0.117	0.118	0.153
Chile	0.223	0.200	0.199	0.200	0.238
China	0.781	0.748	0.747	0.749	0.803
Hong Kong	0.030	0.030	0.030	0.030	0.030
India	0.958	0.921	0.920	0.922	0.982
Indonesia	0.958	0.921	0.920	0.922	0.982
Japan	0.151	0.129	0.129	0.130	0.165
Korea	0.232	0.209	0.208	0.210	0.247
Malaysia	0.268	0.245	0.244	0.245	0.284
Mexico	0.420	0.394	0.393	0.394	0.438
New Zealand	0.028	0.016	0.022	0.009	0.040
Peru	0.337	0.312	0.311	0.313	0.353
Philippines	0.529	0.500	0.499	0.501	0.548
Singapore	0.030	0.030	0.030	0.030	0.030
Taiwan	0.191	0.168	0.168	0.169	0.205
Thailand	0.420	0.394	0.393	0.394	0.438
United States	0.045	0.031	0.036	0.026	0.058
Vietnam	0.574	0.544	0.544	0.545	0.593
Other ASEAN	0.469	0.442	0.441	0.442	0.487
Russia	0.489	0.461	0.461	0.462	0.508
European Union	0.051	0.037	0.041	0.032	0.064
Rest of world	0.218	0.199	0.199	0.198	0.231

Source: Based on gravity model regression studies of service trade flows conducted by Wang, Mohan, and Rosen (2009). These estimates are the sum of country and sector dummy variables estimated by the regressions. Some missing cells were filled in with data from similar economies.

for each type of NTB. These factors are multiplied together to yield NTB reduction factors:

$$r = \lambda * P * S, \tag{D.2}$$

where r = NTB reduction factors $(N_i \times N_a)$,
λ = maximum NTB reduction rates (diagonal matrix $N_i \times N_i$),
P = policy coefficients that map issue scores into NTB reductions $(N_i \times N_p)$,

S = score (0–1) matrix that measures issue coverage of agreements $(N_p \times N_a)$,

N_i = number of NTB categories = 2 (goods and services),

N_p = number of policy issue areas = 21, and

N_a = number of agreements = 57 (47 existing and 10 proposed).

The scores matrix S consists of values assigned to agreements in each of the 21 issue areas ranging from 0 to 1. These scores reflect subjective assessments of the coverage of the issue in the agreement, typically based on the extent of the discussion. Since this effort was undertaken, the WTO has published similar scores that could prove valuable in future work (WTO 2011).

The policy coefficient matrix P has rows that sum to 1; its nonzero entries represent policy weights for various issues (that is, FTA provisions) in reducing a particular NTB. At this time, we distinguish only between goods and services NTBs; further distinctions could be made in future work. Most but not all such policy coefficients are positive. A large, positive coefficient means that an issue will have a significant impact on reducing the barrier (for example, the investment issue area has a large role in determining services NTBs). A few coefficients are negative, indicating that high scores on some rules will tend to increase rather than reduce barriers to trade.

To see how this formula works, consider an agreement with perfect scores of 1.0 in all issue areas (the agreements column of the S matrix consists of ones). Then the product $P * S$ will yield a matrix of ones. If we further assume that NTBs can be fully eliminated by policy ($\lambda = 1$), then equation (D.2) yields 100 percent reduction (full elimination) of all NTBs. If only 50 percent of NTBs are assumed to consist of barriers that can be eliminated by trade policy changes ($\lambda = 0.5I$), then the reduction associated with perfect scores will be 50 percent. And if we assume that an agreement is only half-perfect (its column in the S matrix has 0.5 values), then the NTB reductions associated with it will be only 25 percent.

The P and S matrixes used in the simulations are presented in table D.3. The λ factor indicating the maximum potential reduction of NTBs through policies was set at 0.67. The results calculated using equations (D.1) and (D.2) and applied in the simulations—the utilization rates μ and the r matrix—are reported in table 3.2 in chapter 3.

The policy coefficient matrix P in table D.3 shows, for example, that in determining the reductions to be applied to NTBs affecting goods trade, we assign the greatest weight to provisions dealing with tariffs, nontariff measures, government procurement, and competition. These weights are applied to the scores of agreements in each issue area. Examples of such scores (columns of the S matrix) are shown in the right-hand-side columns of table D.3. They indicate significant differences between prior agreements involving the United States and Asian track countries; on average, Asian track scores are only half as high. As might be expected, the prior US scores are especially high relative to the Asian track for social issues such as labor and the environment.

Table D.3 Policy weights and scores for trade agreements

| Issue area | Assigned policy weights (percent) | | | Average scores | |
	Goods NTBs	Services NTBs	FDI barriers	Recent United States	Recent ASEAN
1 Tariffs	13.0	0	0	0.97	0.89
2 Nontariff measures	13.0	0	0	0.91	0.53
3 E-commerce	4.3	15.8	4.0	0.97	0.26
4 State-owned enterprises	0	0	0	0.84	0.20
5 Agriculture	4.3	0	0	1.00	0.48
6 Rules of origin	0	0	0	0.99	0.68
7 Customs	8.7	0	8.0	0.94	0.54
8 Sanitary and phytosanitary measures	8.7	0	8.0	0.62	0.67
9 Technical barriers to trade	8.7	10.5	8.0	0.90	0.65
10 Trade remedies	−8.7	−5.3	0	0.97	0.53
11 Government procurement	13.0	15.8	12.0	0.89	0.15
12 Investment	8.7	15.8	16.0	0.98	0.73
13 Services	4.3	21.1	12.0	0.72	0.30
14 Competition	13.0	15.8	8.0	0.94	0.37
15 Intellectual property rights	8.7	0	12.0	1.00	0.26
16 Labor	−8.7	−5.3	0	0.95	0.04
17 Environment	8.7	0	0	1.00	0.62
18 Dispute resolution	8.7	5.3	0	0.74	0.81
19 Cooperation	4.3	5.3	4.0	0	0.56
20 Small and medium enterprises	4.3	5.3	4.0	0.00	0.06
21 Science and technology	0	0	4.0	0.08	0.13
Sum/average	100.0	100.0	100.0	0.78	0.45

Source: Authors' estimates.

Asian scores are higher for only a few issues, such as science and technology and small and medium enterprises. Neither track has much prior experience with provisions on safety standards, logistics, and culture. These differences in scores, when weighted by the coefficients of the P matrix, explain the larger NTB reductions applied in simulations of the TPP track (53 percent) than of the Asian track (36 percent), as reported in table 3.2.

The results presented in table 3.2 show the final parameter changes that result from the full implementation of an agreement. Each agreement is assumed to be implemented over five years (with 20 percent of the reduction applied in the first year, 40 percent in the second year, and so on) beginning in the year that it comes into force. In cases where a bilateral trade flow is subject to multiple agreements, the largest of projected reductions is used.

Costs Associated with Meeting Rules of Origin

For the most part, FTAs lower barriers and improve productivity. However, trade diversion to inefficient regional suppliers works in the opposite direction. Such effects are automatically taken into account by CGE simulations, since all sourcing decisions (by households purchasing consumption goods and by industries purchasing inputs) respond to relative prices that incorporate the effects of preferential barriers. One effect, however, is not automatically modeled: A firm may incur additional costs in order to qualify its exports for preferential tariffs. These additional costs include the administrative burden of meeting ROO certification, but more importantly they may involve using costlier domestic or regional inputs in order to satisfy ROO requirements.

We represent these costs by *adding* iceberg costs to bilateral trade flows within an FTA. The size of the productivity penalty is assumed to depend on the size of the tariff preference, since this is the benefit of meeting the ROO. We calculate the penalty attached to each bilateral trade flow using the formula:

$$q = \delta * \mu * \Delta t, \tag{D.3}$$

where q = productivity cost of meeting ROO,
δ = loss factor,
μ = utilization rate of the tariff preference, and
Δt = preferential tariff reduction.

The loss factor δ is set to ½ for small agreements but is assumed to decline to 0 for large agreements such as the FTAAP, since in that setting regional sourcing options should permit fully efficient input decisions.

Appendix E
Quantifying the Investment
Effects of Agreements

Trade agreements reduce barriers to FDI by ensuring national treatment, easing ownership restrictions, and protecting investors' intellectual property and other assets, in part through rigorous dispute resolution procedures. These measures increase returns on existing foreign investment and stimulate additional investment. They also cut rents earned by investors and hosts (if any) and reduce costs imposed by regulatory requirements.

Modern FDI theory has been built into some general equilibrium models using industry-detailed equations (Petri 1997, Dee and Hanslow 2001). However, the FDI relationships add considerable complexity and have large, hard-to-meet data requirements. Since modeling trade flows in a heterogeneous firms setting is already much more complex than the usual CGE approach, we elected to avoid further modeling detail and use a simple and mostly exogenous approach to represent FDI effects. The approach is based on a gravity specification to project baseline FDI stocks and uses econometric estimates to judge how reductions in barriers due to trade agreements affect FDI stocks. Benefits are based on the estimated FDI changes.

The FDI side model consists of three components. First, we construct a baseline projection of bilateral FDI stocks to 2025. Second, we estimate the effects of trade agreements on the bilateral stocks. Third, we calculate the welfare effects of FDI changes. These steps are reviewed below.

Baseline FDI Projections

The bilateral matrix of FDI stocks in 2010 is based on the IMF's Coordinated Direct Investment Survey (IMF 2010). When available, inward (host) and outward (investor) estimates of a bilateral stock were averaged. Some elements of the stock matrix were adjusted to reallocate investments that flow through the tax havens of the Bahamas and the Cayman Islands and to eliminate counting as FDI the "round trip" investments of Chinese firms in China through Hong Kong.

The stock matrix was projected forward using the gravity equation:

$$F_{ij}^t = F_{ij}^{2010}(Y_i^t/Y_i^{2010})^\alpha \, (Y_j^t/Y_j^{2010})^\alpha, \tag{E.1}$$

where F_{ij}^t is the stock of investment by country i in country j at time t, Y_i^t is the GDP of country i at time t, and α is the gravity exponent on GDP, set to 1.09, based on estimates for the Peterson Institute gravity model by Dean DeRosa and Gary Clyde Hufbauer (Hufbauer 2010, appendix tables I.4 and I.5).

Under these assumptions, the global FDI stock—the sum of the projected bilateral stock matrix—will grow at an annual rate of 7.3 percent between 2010 and 2025, almost twice as fast as world output but slower than the 12 percent (nominal) average growth rate during 1990–2010. The projections show global FDI stocks expanding from $19 trillion in 2010 (33 percent of world GDP) to $56 trillion in 2025 (55 percent of world GDP). If these projections hold, FDI will play an increasingly important role in international linkages.

Effects of Trade Agreements on FDI

The effects of trade agreements on bilateral FDI stocks are estimated as a product of (1) the *potential increase* in inward FDI stocks in each economy and (2) the barrier *reduction factor* associated with a trade agreement. The product of these factors determines how much FDI moves toward its potential.

Estimates of investment potential are based on the equation reported in table E.1, which presents a simple cross-section regression of inward FDI stocks on GDP, GDP per capita, and a proxy for the investment climate (the World Bank's Doing Business rank). The estimation is based on 2010 data for 169 countries. All coefficients are highly significant. The coefficient of the investment climate variable has the expected sign and suggests that advancing 10 percent in the global Doing Business rankings (say, moving up nine positions near the middle of the distribution) increases inward FDI by 2.2 percent.

The potential increase of each bilateral inward FDI stock is estimated from two components: an "explained potential" that consists of additional inward stocks that would result from improvements in the measured investment climate of the host country and an "unexplained potential" that consists of increases that could be achieved if the gap between the host country's inward stocks and international norms were reduced. For well-performing countries either or both can be zero. The explained potential is estimated by lifting a country's Doing Business rank to the 90th percentile. Some countries, such as Hong Kong and the United States, are already above this level, so have no explained potential. The unexplained potential is estimated as closing *half* the

Table E.1 Regression equations for FDI stocks

Variable	Coefficient
Intercept	5.38 (6.81)
ln(GDP)	0.79 (23.79)
ln(GDP/Pop)	0.25 (4.08)
ln(Doing Business rank)	−0.22 (−2.42)

Dependent variable: ln(inward FDI stock)
N = 169, adjusted R^2 = 0.89, F = 438; t-ratios in parentheses.

Source: Authors' estimates.

gap (if positive) between a country's FDI stock and the regression prediction for that country. Some countries, such as Singapore and Vietnam, are already above regression predictions, so have no unexplained potential. Potential increase estimates are reported in table 4.3 in chapter 4.

The FDI increase realized due to a trade agreement is calculated as a fraction of the potential determined by the score of FDI provisions of the agreement:

$$f_{ij}^a = \theta s_j^a g_j^{pot} F_{ij}, \tag{E.2}$$

where f_{ij}^a is the increase in the bilateral FDI stock from investor i to host j under agreement a, θ is the maximum reduction in barriers achievable through policy (set to 2/3), s_j^a is the score of the FDI-related provisions accepted by host j under agreement a (as explained in appendix C), g_j^{pot} is the potential increase in FDI, and F_{ij} is the baseline bilateral FDI stock. For example, an agreement with an FDI liberalization score of 0.6 will increase FDI by 40 percent (0.6 × 2/3) of the potential increase estimated for the host economy. FDI liberalization is assumed to affect only the bilateral stocks covered by an agreement, although in practice some liberalization measures are likely to benefit other investors too. When multiple agreements cover a bilateral FDI stock, the one with the higher (more liberal) score is assumed to apply.

Welfare Effects

Welfare effects of investment liberalization—annual income gains generated by changes in FDI stocks—are estimated using a partial equilibrium supply-demand framework. The inward FDI market is assumed to be subject to barriers that create a "wedge" between returns in the host country and returns to foreign investors. The wedge consists of rents and inefficiency losses.

Let $D(q)$ represent the returns to investment in the host country and $S(q)$ represent the returns received by the foreign investors, both at a given

Figure E.1   Implications of investment barriers

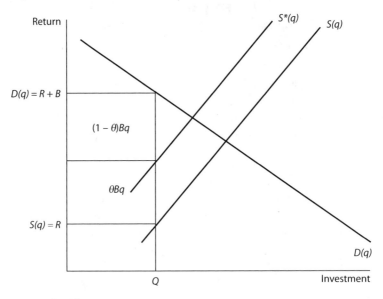

Source: Authors' illustration.

investment level q with country subscripts suppressed. The difference (wedge) between these returns is the barrier to FDI (B):

$$D(q) - S(q) = B \tag{E.3}$$

Differentiating equation (E.3) shows how the barrier has to change to increase q by dq:

$$\frac{dB}{dq} = D'(q) - S'(q) = [(R+B)/\varepsilon^D - R/\varepsilon^S]/q \tag{E.4}$$

Here ε^D and ε^S are the elasticities of demand and supply of foreign investment, and $R = S(q)$ is the return earned by foreign investors.

The total welfare (or surplus) associated with a bilateral investment activity is given by:

$$W = \int_0^Q D(q)dq - \int_0^Q S(q)dq - \theta Bq \tag{E.5}$$

As figure E.1 shows, welfare is the area between the demand and supply curves, less the inefficiency losses created by barriers. As an agreement reduces barriers, it increases FDI and generates more surplus. Inefficiency losses also decline (at least per unit of investment). The derivative of welfare with respect to the quantity of investment is:

$$\frac{dW}{dq} = D(q) - S(q) - \theta B - \theta q \frac{dB}{dq} \tag{E.6}$$

The first three terms of equation E.6 represent an increase in rents (due to more investment) and the fourth term represents reduced efficiency losses (due to liberalization).

The derivative dB/dq is given by equation E.4 and is negative because normally $\varepsilon^D < 0$ and $\varepsilon^S > 0$. Combining equations (E.4) and (E.6):

$$\frac{dW}{dq} = (1 - \theta - \theta/\varepsilon^D)B - \theta\left[\frac{1}{\varepsilon^D} - \frac{1}{\varepsilon^S}\right]R \qquad (E.7)$$

Equation E.7 yields coefficients for estimating the welfare effects of FDI changes that result from liberalization. For example, $R = 0.25$, $B = 0.25/3$, $\theta = 0.5$, and $-\varepsilon^D = \varepsilon^S = 1$ implies $dW/dq = 1/3$, the total benefit coefficient we used in simulations. Assuming also that benefits are split evenly between investing and host countries, this yields benefit coefficients of 1/6 for both outward and inward changes in FDI stocks. Note that these coefficients measure annual *excess* returns—surpluses generated in the foreign investment process—not gross returns.

The analysis is illustrated in figure E.1. $D(q)$ and $S(q)$ are returns in the host market and to investors at an investment level q. $S^*(q)$ is the return required in the host market after inefficiency losses (θBq). The rectangle $(1 - \theta)Bq$ measures rents earned by investors and the host country. The welfare associated with FDI (as given in equation E.5) is the area below the D curve and above the S^* curve; it includes rents plus surpluses to investors and host.

Appendix F
Model Sensitivity

Any CGE model contains many assumptions and estimated parameters, and the more advanced model we use in this study includes more than most. Potential sources of error include base year data, the specification of the model, and the specification of scenarios. Sensitivity analysis can identify the parameters that matter most to key results—especially trade and welfare effects—and provide a bracket for likely estimates. This appendix reports on several approaches for assessing the errors implicit in the estimates. None of these approaches produces a comprehensive estimate of errors and our work to develop sensitivity results continues.

Assessing CGE errors is complicated by the fact that even when information is available on errors in individual parameters (say, from econometric studies), there is seldom evidence on covariances among these errors. This evidence would be needed to judge to what extent errors in different parts of the model will cumulate or cancel in affecting aggregate results. But since the assumptions and estimates of the model combine information on very different mechanisms from multiple, unrelated sources, it is reasonable to expect significant canceling of errors.

Errors in *basic economic data* are likely to be small compared with errors that arise in the behavioral parameters (e.g., elasticities) that drive the simulations. GTAP's data system incorporates recent information from major, commonly used statistical sources. Much of this information—on national income and trade—is now reported fairly accurately for many countries. The "social accounting matrix" methodology of GTAP also imposes consistency checks and forces adjustments that are likely to improve the estimates.

Errors in *scenario specification* can be evaluated by simulating multiple scenarios. An important potential source of error is the scoring assumptions used to describe the nontariff barriers of past and prospective agreements, as discussed in appendix C. The methodology we use to make these estimates does not generate confidence intervals, so other means have to be used to assess validity. One way to judge validity is to see how much difference these assumptions make in simulations, other features of the model being held constant. The analysis of the FTAAP scenario in this study provides an example: The model structure and the membership of the agreement are held constant, and only the scores applied to simulate different templates are varied. The results are presented in table 5.3 in chapter 5 and provide a measure of how much difference can be attributed to wide variations in liberalization estimates (presumably greater than those due to error alone). Overall, the variation in the liberalization templates (the difference between the TPP and Asian templates) changes estimated benefits by 57 percent of the average estimate. Half of the estimated changes for different economies were in the 47 to 67 percent range. If one assumes that unintended errors are, say, one-third as large as the observed difference between distant observations, the error in benefit estimates would be +/– 19 percent.

Errors in *model specification* are even harder to assess, but to some extent can be tested by changing structural parameters. Three sets of parameters are particularly important to the results: elasticities of substitution of different varieties of goods, parameters that describe the distribution of productivity across firms, and assumptions about the role of fixed costs associated with international trade. Zhai (2008) reports sensitivity results for these parameters using a model that is structurally similar to the one applied in this study. In each case, he examines how parameter changes affect predictions for the effects of trade liberalization—in those experiments, a 50 percent cut in MFN tariffs by all world regions. He examines this policy scenario with a base model and then with models based on alternative parameters.

First, he changes the elasticity of substitution among varieties by +/– 1/3—a magnitude similar to the standard error estimated in econometric studies. This changes the income gains estimated from liberalization by +/– 10 percent and trade gains by +/– 7.5 percent.[1] Second, he reduces by 1/3 a parameter that determines heterogeneity in firm productivity (in effect, he makes firms more homogeneous). This reduces the estimated welfare and trade effects of liberalization by about 1/3.[2] Third, he changes parameters that determine the division of trade costs between fixed and variable costs in calibrating the model. In this case, he finds negligible effects on income and trade

---

1. In the Melitz framework, a variety-loving (low substitution elasticity) economy benefits from more trade from liberalization than a variety-shunning economy, because liberalization improves access to foreign varieties.

2. The logic is that interfirm shifts caused by trade liberalization have more limited productivity benefits.

predictions. In sum, Zhai (2008) finds that reasonable changes in parameters can change results by zero to as much as 1/3 of their initial value.

Another possible specification issue involves assumptions about how liberalization affects protection. In heterogeneous firm trade theory, barriers to trade involve variable trade costs, fixed trade costs, or both. Currently available estimates of trade barriers were not developed in this theoretical framework, and therefore assumptions have to be made about what types of barriers they represent. In applying these estimates, we assume that trade barriers affect both variable and fixed costs equally and that liberalization therefore reduces both types of costs. (Some provisions in trade agreements are explicitly designed to lower fixed trade costs, including efforts to make information about trade opportunities, regulations, and transactions more transparent and easily accessible.)

Which barriers are liberalized matters because lower fixed trade costs have a particularly strong effect on the extensive margin of trade. If only variable trade costs are reduced, the effects of liberalization affect primarily the intensive margin of trade, that is, increase the exports of firms that already export. This assumption yields results similar to those of standard CGE models, which rely on the Armington assumption to determine trade flows. Table F.1 shows the effect of using such assumptions, that is, the share of the total estimated effects that are accounted for by variable cost only liberalization. With this specification—similar to that used in conventional CGE models—total benefits would be about half as large as under our standard assumptions, with both fixed and variable trade costs reduced.[3] The share of variable trade cost effects is especially low for the TPP, indicating that the extensive margin trade plays a large role in the context of the TPP template

A comparative perspective on model errors is offered by the USITC's (2010) general equilibrium study of the Korea-US Free Trade Agreement. That study uses a somewhat different model (a single-period GTAP model with a more conventional trade structure) and conducts sensitivity analysis by changing substitution elasticities by one standard deviation. (In that model these elasticities apply to domestic and imported varieties.) The results change estimated welfare and trade effects by roughly +/- 7.5 percent from those computed with their standard model. The current model is likely to have a larger error range because it incorporates more channels of trade effects. The emerging professional consensus, backed by a rapidly expanding empirical literature, is that firm heterogeneity effects such as those incorporated in the present model are important in evaluating the gains from trade.

There is no simple way to integrate these disparate findings. It appears that insignificant or modest errors in results—under 10 percent—are likely to result from errors in basic data and in elasticities of substitution among

---

3. For both variable and fixed costs, only 2/3 of estimated barriers are assumed to be subject to policy measures. In other words, a maximum of 2/3 of barriers would be eliminated under trade agreements with scores of 1.0 on all relevant provisions.

Table F.1 Share of variable cost effects in total trade effects

Economy	TPP track	Asian track	Both tracks	FTAAP
TPP track economies	0.28	0.77	0.31	0.35
United States	0.19	1.09	0.23	0.27
Australia	0.09	0.09	0.10	0.30
Canada	0.21	0.75	0.23	0.26
Chile	0.27	—	0.26	0.31
Mexico	0.52	0.66	0.54	0.59
New Zealand	0.25	0.32	0.26	0.31
Peru	0.42	0.69	0.42	0.43
Asian track economies	0.38	0.47	0.49	0.58
China	0.38	0.45	0.48	0.60
Hong Kong	0.36	0.51	0.52	0.49
Indonesia	0.46	0.52	0.54	0.54
Philippines	0.45	0.62	0.65	0.59
Thailand	0.39	0.48	0.53	0.48
Two-track economies	0.39	0.46	0.43	0.44
Brunei	0.40	0.59	0.50	0.48
Japan	0.35	0.46	0.40	0.40
Korea	0.38	0.43	0.43	0.42
Malaysia	0.34	0.48	0.38	0.41
Singapore	0.21	0.59	—	0.14
Vietnam	0.56	0.74	0.59	0.67
Other	0.36	0.59	0.47	0.54
Russia	0.37	0.62	0.52	0.62
Taiwan	0.44	0.62	0.59	0.39
Europe	—	0.86	—	0.62
India	0.34	0.62	0.54	0.55
Other ASEAN	0.52	0.54	0.56	0.58
Rest of world	0.49	0.91	0.55	0.69
World	0.35	0.46	0.43	0.50
Memorandum				
TPP	0.33	0.67	0.37	0.37
ASEAN+3	0.39	0.46	0.45	0.53
APEC	0.34	0.46	0.43	0.51

— = the effect changes sign with variable cost liberalization.

Source: Authors' calculations.

varieties. Intermediate-scale errors—in the 20 to 33 percent range—are probably associated with the specification of liberalization scenarios and assumptions about the extent of heterogeneity among firms. Finally, larger errors—perhaps up to 50 percent or more—might result from how liberalization is implemented in the model, and in particular whether or not fixed cost barriers are reduced. These several errors involve different features of the model and are therefore not likely to co-vary. An overall error range of +/– 1/3 offers a plausible summary of these considerations.

References

Aggarwal, Vinod L., and Seungjoo Lee, eds. 2011. *Trade Policy in the Asia-Pacific: The Role of Ideas, Interests, and Domestic Institutions.* New York: Springer.

APEC (Asia Pacific Economic Cooperation forum). 2010. *2010 Leaders' Declaration.* Available at www.apec.org/Meeting-Papers/Leaders-Declarations/2010/2010_aelm.aspx (accessed on September 11, 2012).

Athukorala, Prema-chandra, and Archanun Kohpaiboon. 2011. Australian-Thai Trade: Has the Free Trade Agreement Made a Difference? *Australian Economic Review* 44, no. 4 (December): 457-67.

Baldwin, R. E. 1995. A Domino Theory of Regionalism. In *Expanding Membership of the European Union*, ed. R. E. Baldwin, P. Haaparanta, and J. Kiander. Cambridge, UK: Cambridge University Press.

Baldwin, R. E. 2006. Multilateralising Regionalism: Spaghetti Bowls as Building Blocs on the Path to Global Free Trade. *World Economy* 29: 1451-518.

Barfield, Claude. 2011. The Trans-Pacific Partnership: A Model for Twenty-First-Century Trade Agreements? *AEI International Economic Outlook,* no. 2 (June): 1-8.

Bergsten, C. Fred, and William R. Cline. 1983. Trade Policy in the 1980s: An Overview. In *Trade Policy in the 1980s,* ed. William R. Cline. Washington: Institute for International Economics.

Bergsten, C. Fred, and Jeffrey J. Schott. 2010. *Submission to the USTR in Support of a Trans-Pacific Partnership Agreement* (January 25). Washington: Peterson Institute for International Economics.

Bora, Bijit, Aki Kuwahara, and Sam Laird. 2002. *Quantification of Non-Tariff Measures.* Policy Issues in International Trade and Commodities Study Series 18. Geneva: United Nations Conference on Trade and Development.

Dee, P., and K. Hanslow. 2001. Multilateral Liberalization of Services Trade. In *Services in the International Economy,* ed. R. Stern. Ann Arbor: University of Michigan Press.

Eaton, Jonathan, Samuel Kortum, and Francis Kramarz. 2004. Dissecting Trade: Firms, Industries, and Export Destinations. *American Economic Review* 94, no. 2 (May): 150-54.

Elms, Deborah K. 2009. From the P4 to the TPP: Explaining Expansion Interests in the Asia-Pacific. Paper presented at the ESCAP Trade Economists Conference, Bangkok, November 2–3.

Fergusson, Ian F. 2008. *World Trade Organization Negotiations: The Doha Development Agenda.* CRS Report RL32060 (January 18). Washington: Congressional Research Service.

Fergusson, Ian F., and Bruce Vaughn. 2009. *The Trans-Pacific Strategic Economic Partnership Agreement.* CRS Report R40502 (December 7). Washington: Congressional Research Service.

Feridhanusetyawan, Tubagus. 2005. *Preferential Trade Agreements in the Asia-Pacific Region.* IMF Working Paper WP/05/149. Washington: International Monetary Fund.

Findlay, Christopher, and Shujiro Urata, eds. 2010. *Free Trade Agreements in the Asia Pacific.* World Scientific Studies in International Economics, volume 11. New Jersey: World Scientific.

Fink, Carsten. 2009. *Has the EU's Single Market Program Led to Deeper Integration of EU Services Markets?* Working Paper. Paris: SciencesPo.

Fouré, Jean, Agnès Bénassy-Quéré, and Lionel Fontagné. 2010. *The World Economy in 2050: A Tentative Picture 2010–27.* Paris: CEPII.

Frankel, Jeffrey, Ernesto Stein, and Shang-jin Wei. 1995. Trading Blocs and the Americas: The Natural, the Unnatural, and the Supernatural. *Journal of Development Economics* 47, no. 1 (June): 61–95.

Friedberg, Aaron L. 2011. Hegemony with Chinese Characteristics. *National Interest* (June 21): 18–27.

Helble, Matthias, Ben Shepherd, and John S. Wilson. 2007. Transparency and Trade Facilitation in the Asia Pacific: Estimating the Gains from Reform. Manuscript (June). Washington: World Bank.

Hufbauer, Gary Clyde. 2010. *Three Scenarios for the World Economy 2010 to 2020: Implications for Trade Policy and Social Indicators.* Report to the National Intelligence Council (March 23). Washington: Peterson Institute for International Economics.

Hufbauer, Gary Clyde, Jeffrey J. Schott, and Woan Foong Wong. 2010. *Figuring Out the Doha Round.* Policy Analyses in International Economics 91. Washington: Peterson Institute for International Economics.

Hummels, David, and Peter J. Klenow. 2005. The Variety and Quality of a Nation's Exports. *American Economic Review* 95, no. 3: 704–23.

IMF (International Monetary Fund). 2010. *The Coordinated Direct Investment Survey Guide.* Washington.

Itakura, Ken, and Hiro Lee. 2012. *Welfare Changes and Sectoral Adjustments of Asia-Pacific Countries under Alternative Sequencings of Free-Trade Agreements.* OSIPP Discussion Paper DP-2012-E-005 (March 30). Osaka School of International Public Policy, Osaka University.

Kawai, Masahiro, and Ganeshan Wignaraja. 2008. *Regionalism as an Engine of Multilateralism: A Case for a Single East Asian FTA.* Working Paper Series 14. Manila: Asian Development Bank.

Kawai, Masahiro, and Ganeshan Wignaraja, eds. 2011. *Asia's Free Trade Agreements: How Is Business Responding?* Cheltenham, UK: Edward Elgar.

Kawasaki, Kenichi. 2010. *The Macro and Sectoral Significance of an FTAAP.* ESRI Discussion Paper Series no. 244. Tokyo: Economic and Social Research Institute, Cabinet Office.

Kee, Hiau Looi, Alessandro Nicita, and Marcelo Olarreaga. 2009. Estimating Trade Restrictiveness Indices. *Economic Journal* 119: 172–99.

Kehoe, Timothy J. 2005. An Evaluation of the Performance of Applied General Equilibrium Models on the Impact of NAFTA. In *Frontiers in Applied General Equilibrium Modeling: In Honor of Herbert Scarf,* ed. T. J. Kehoe, T. N. Srinivasan, and J. Whalley. Cambridge, UK: Cambridge University Press.

Kehoe, Timothy J., and Kim J. Ruhl. 2003. *How Important Is the New Goods Margin in International Trade?* Staff Report 324. Minneapolis: Federal Reserve Bank of Minneapolis.

Li, Chunding, and John Whalley. 2012. *China and the TPP: A Numerical Simulation Assessment of the Effects Involved.* NBER Working Paper 18090 (May). Cambridge, MA: National Bureau of Economic Research.

Lieberthal, Kenneth, and Wang Jisi. 2012. *Addressing US-China Strategic Distrust.* John L. Thornton Monograph Series 4. Washington: Brookings Institution.

Maddison, Angus. 2001. *The World Economy: A Millennial Perspective.* Development Centre Studies. Paris: Organization for Economic Cooperation and Development.

McCulloch, Rachel, and Peter A. Petri. 1997. Alternative Paths Toward Open Global Markets. In *Quiet Pioneering: Robert M. Stern and His International Economic Legacy,* ed. Keith E. Maskus, Peter M. Hooper, Edward E. Leamer, and J. David Richardson. Ann Arbor: University of Michigan Press.

Melitz, Marc J. 2003. The Impact of Trade on Intra-Industry Reallocations and Aggregate Industry Productivity. *Econometrica* 71, no. 6: 1695–725.

Park, Innwon. 2006. East Asian Regional Trade Agreements: Do They Promote Global Free Trade? *Pacific Economic Review* 11, no. 4: 547–68.

Park, Innwon, Soonchan Park, and Sangkyom Kim. 2010. *A Free Trade Area of the Asia Pacific (FTAAP): Is It Desirable?* MPRA Paper 26680. Available at http://mpra.ub.uni-muenchen.de/26680 (accessed on September 11, 2012).

Petri, Peter A. 1997. *Foreign Direct Investment in a Computable General Equilibrium Framework.* Brandeis International Business School. Paper prepared for conference on Making APEC Work: Economic Challenges and Policy Alternatives, Keio University, Tokyo, March 13–14. Available at http://papers.ssrn.com/sol3/papers.cfm?abstract_id=1549616 (accessed on September 11, 2012).

Petri, Peter A., and Michael G. Plummer. 2012. *The Trans-Pacific Partnership and Asia-Pacific Integration: Policy Implications.* Policy Briefs in International Economics 12-16. Washington: Peterson Institute for International Economics.

Petri, Peter A., Michael G. Plummer, and Fan Zhai. 2012. The ASEAN Economic Community: A General Equilibrium Analysis. *Asian Economic Journal* 26, no. 2: 93–118.

Petri, Peter A., and Fan Zhai. 2012. *Navigating a Changing World Economy: ASEAN, the PRC and India, 2010–2030.* Background Paper for the Great Transformation Study. Tokyo: Asian Development Bank Institute.

Plummer, Michael G., and Chia Siow Yue, eds. 2009. *Realizing the ASEAN Economic Community: A Comprehensive Assessment.* Singapore: Institute of Southeast Asian Studies.

Productivity Commission (Australia). 2010. *Bilateral and Regional Trade Agreements.* Research Report. Canberra.

Ravenhill, John. 2009. Extending the TPP: The Political Economy of Multilateralization in Asia. Paper presented at the ESCAP Trade Economists Conference, Bangkok, November 2–3.

Ricardo, David. 1817. *On the Principles of Political Economy and Taxation.* London: John Murray. Available at www.econlib.org/library/Ricardo/ricP.html (accessed on September 11, 2012).

Scollay, Robert, and John Gilbert. 2000. Measuring the Gains from APEC Trade Liberalisation: An Overview of CGE Assessments. *World Economy* 23, no. 2: 175–97.

USITC (United States International Trade Commission). 2010. *US-Korea Free Trade Agreement: Potential Economy-wide and Selected Sectoral Effects.* Investigation No. TA-2104-24. Washington.

USTR (United States Trade Representative). 2011a. *Engagement with the Trans-Pacific Partnership to Increase Exports, Support Jobs.* Washington. Available at www.ustr.gov/about-us/press-office/

fact-sheets/2011/february/engagement-Trans-Pacific-partnership-increase-export (accessed on September 11, 2012).

USTR (United States Trade Representative). 2011b. *Outlines of the Trans-Pacific Partnership Agreement* (November 12). Washington. Available at www.ustr.gov/about-us/press-office/fact-sheets/2011/november/outlines-trans-pacific-partnership-agreement (accessed on September 11, 2012).

Wang, Zhi, Shashank Mohan, and Daniel Rosen. 2009. Methodology for Estimating Services Barriers. Rhodium Group and Peterson Institute for International Economics. Unpublished. On file with authors.

WTO (World Trade Organization). 2008. *Trans-Pacific Strategic Economic Partnership Agreement between Brunei Darussalam, Chile, New Zealand and Singapore (Goods and Services)*. Document WT/REG229/1. Geneva.

WTO (World Trade Organization). 2011. *World Trade Report 2011—The WTO and preferential trade agreements: From co-existence to coherence*. Geneva.

Zhai, Fan. 2008. Armington Meets Melitz: Introducing Firm Heterogeneity in a Global CGE Model of Trade. *Journal of Economic Integration* 23, no. 3 (September): 575–604.

Zhiming, Xin. 2011. North Asia Free-Trade Area Agreement Enormously Beneficial but Years Away. *China Daily*, September 1.

Abbreviations

AANZFTA	ASEAN-Australia-New Zealand Free Trade Agreement
ACTA	Anti-Counterfeiting Trade Agreement
ADB-ARIC	Asian Development Bank, Asia Regional Integration Center
AFTA	ASEAN Free Trade Area
APEC	Asia-Pacific Economic Cooperation forum
ASEAN	Association of Southeast Asian Nations
BITs	bilateral investment treaties
CEPII	Centre d'Etudes Prospectives et d'Informations Internationales
CES	constant elasticity of substitution
CGE	computable general equilibrium model
CITES	Convention on International Trade in Endangered Species of Wild Fauna and Flora
EPA	Economic Partnership Agreement (Japan)
ESCAP	United Nations Economic and Social Commission for Asia and the Pacific
FDI	foreign direct investment
FTA	free trade agreement
FTAAP	Free Trade Area of the Asia Pacific
GTAP	Global Trade Analysis Project
ILO	International Labor Organization
IMF	International Monetary Fund
IPRs	intellectual property rights
MFN	most favored nation
NAFTA	North American Free Trade Agreement
NTBs	nontariff barriers

OECD	Organization for Economic Cooperation and Development
P4	Pacific 4 (Trans-Pacific Strategic Economic Partnership Agreement between Brunei Darussalam, Chile, Singapore, and New Zealand)
RCEP	Regional Comprehensive Economic Partnership
ROO	rules of origin
SMEs	small and medium enterprises
SOEs	state-owned enterprises
SPS	sanitary and phytosanitary measures
TBT	technical barriers to trade
TPP	Trans-Pacific Partnership
TRIPS	WTO's Agreement on Trade-Related Aspects of Intellectual Property Rights
WIPO	World Intellectual Property Organization
WTO	World Trade Organization

Index

Other Publications from the
Peterson Institute for International Economics

POLICY BRIEFS

* = out of print

POLICY ANALYSES IN INTERNATIONAL ECONOMICS Series

International Adjustment and Financing: The Lessons of 1985-1991*   C. Fred Bergsten, ed.
January 1992   ISBN 0-88132-112-5
North American Free Trade: Issues and Recommendations*   Gary Clyde Hufbauer and Jeffrey J. Schott
April 1992   ISBN 0-88132-120-6
Narrowing the U.S. Current Account Deficit*   Alan J. Lenz
June 1992   ISBN 0-88132-103-6
The Economics of Global Warming   William R. Cline
June 1992   ISBN 0-88132-132-X
US Taxation of International Income: Blueprint for Reform   Gary Clyde Hufbauer, assisted by Joanna M. van Rooij
October 1992   ISBN 0-88132-134-6
Who's Bashing Whom? Trade Conflict in High-Technology Industries   Laura D'Andrea Tyson
November 1992   ISBN 0-88132-106-0
Korea in the World Economy*   Il SaKong
January 1993   ISBN 0-88132-183-4
Pacific Dynamism and the International Economic System*   C. Fred Bergsten and Marcus Noland, eds.
May 1993   ISBN 0-88132-196-6
Economic Consequences of Soviet Disintegration*   John Williamson, ed.
May 1993   ISBN 0-88132-190-7
Reconcilable Differences? United States-Japan Economic Conflict*   C. Fred Bergsten and Marcus Noland
June 1993   ISBN 0-88132-129-X
Does Foreign Exchange Intervention Work?   Kathryn M. Dominguez and Jeffrey A. Frankel
September 1993   ISBN 0-88132-104-4
Sizing Up U.S. Export Disincentives*   J. David Richardson
September 1993   ISBN 0-88132-107-9
NAFTA: An Assessment   Gary Clyde Hufbauer and Jeffrey J. Schott, *rev. ed.*
October 1993   ISBN 0-88132-199-0
Adjusting to Volatile Energy Prices   Philip K. Verleger, Jr.
November 1993   ISBN 0-88132-069-2
The Political Economy of Policy Reform   John Williamson, ed.
January 1994   ISBN 0-88132-195-8
Measuring the Costs of Protection in the United States   Gary Clyde Hufbauer and Kimberly Ann Elliott
January 1994   ISBN 0-88132-108-7
The Dynamics of Korean Economic Development*   Cho Soon
March 1994   ISBN 0-88132-162-1
Reviving the European Union*   C. Randall Henning, Eduard Hochreiter, and Gary Clyde Hufbauer, eds.
April 1994   ISBN 0-88132-208-3
China in the World Economy   Nicholas R. Lardy
April 1994   ISBN 0-88132-200-8
Greening the GATT: Trade, Environment, and the Future   Daniel C. Esty
July 1994   ISBN 0-88132-205-9

Western Hemisphere Economic Integration*   Gary Clyde Hufbauer and Jeffrey J. Schott
July 1994   ISBN 0-88132-159-1
Currencies and Politics in the United States, Germany, and Japan   C. Randall Henning
September 1994   ISBN 0-88132-127-3
Estimating Equilibrium Exchange Rates   John Williamson, ed.
September 1994   ISBN 0-88132-076-5
Managing the World Economy: Fifty Years after Bretton Woods   Peter B. Kenen, ed.
September 1994   ISBN 0-88132-212-1
Reciprocity and Retaliation in U.S. Trade Policy   Thomas O. Bayard and Kimberly Ann Elliott
September 1994   ISBN 0-88132-084-6
The Uruguay Round: An Assessment*   Jeffrey J. Schott, assisted by Johanna Buurman
November 1994   ISBN 0-88132-206-7
Measuring the Costs of Protection in Japan*   Yoko Sazanami, Shujiro Urata, and Hiroki Kawai
January 1995   ISBN 0-88132-211-3
Foreign Direct Investment in the United States, 3d ed.   Edward M. Graham and Paul R. Krugman
January 1995   ISBN 0-88132-204-0
The Political Economy of Korea-United States Cooperation*   C. Fred Bergsten and Il SaKong, eds.
February 1995   ISBN 0-88132-213-X
International Debt Reexamined*   William R. Cline
February 1995   ISBN 0-88132-083-8
American Trade Politics, 3d ed.   I. M. Destler
April 1995   ISBN 0-88132-215-6
Managing Official Export Credits: The Quest for a Global Regime*   John E. Ray
July 1995   ISBN 0-88132-207-5
Asia Pacific Fusion: Japan's Role in APEC*   Yoichi Funabashi
October 1995   ISBN 0-88132-224-5
Korea-United States Cooperation in the New World Order*   C. Fred Bergsten and Il SaKong, eds.
February 1996   ISBN 0-88132-226-1
Why Exports Really Matter!*   ISBN 0-88132-221-0
Why Exports Matter More!*   ISBN 0-88132-229-6
J. David Richardson and Karin Rindal
July 1995; February 1996
Global Corporations and National Governments   Edward M. Graham
May 1996   ISBN 0-88132-111-7
Global Economic Leadership and the Group of Seven   C. Fred Bergsten and C. Randall Henning
May 1996   ISBN 0-88132-218-0
The Trading System after the Uruguay Round*   John Whalley and Colleen Hamilton
July 1996   ISBN 0-88132-131-1
Private Capital Flows to Emerging Markets after the Mexican Crisis*   Guillermo A. Calvo, Morris Goldstein, and Eduard Hochreiter
September 1996   ISBN 0-88132-232-6

**Australia, New Zealand,
and Papua New Guinea**
D. A. Information Services
648 Whitehorse Road
Mitcham, Victoria 3132, Australia
Tel: 61-3-9210-7777
Fax: 61-3-9210-7788
Email: service@dadirect.com.au
www.dadirect.com.au

India, Bangladesh, Nepal, and Sri Lanka
Viva Books Private Limited
Mr. Vinod Vasishtha
4737/23 Ansari Road
Daryaganj, New Delhi 110002
India
Tel: 91-11-4224-2200
Fax: 91-11-4224-2240
Email: viva@vivagroupindia.net
www.vivagroupindia.com

**Mexico, Central America, South America,
and Puerto Rico**
US PubRep, Inc.
311 Dean Drive
Rockville, MD 20851
Tel: 301-838-9276
Fax: 301-838-9278
Email: c.falk@ieee.org

Asia *(Brunei, Burma, Cambodia, China,
Hong Kong, Indonesia, Korea, Laos, Malaysia,
Philippines, Singapore, Taiwan, Thailand,
and Vietnam)*
East-West Export Books (EWEB)
University of Hawaii Press
2840 Kolowalu Street
Honolulu, Hawaii 96822-1888
Tel: 808-956-8830
Fax: 808-988-6052
Email: eweb@hawaii.edu

Canada
Renouf Bookstore
5369 Canotek Road, Unit 1
Ottawa, Ontario KlJ 9J3, Canada
Tel: 613-745-2665
Fax: 613-745-7660
www.renoufbooks.com

Japan
United Publishers Services Ltd.
1-32-5, Higashi-shinagawa
Shinagawa-ku, Tokyo 140-0002
Japan
Tel: 81-3-5479-7251
Fax: 81-3-5479-7307
Email: purchasing@ups.co.jp
*For trade accounts only. Individuals will find
Institute books in leading Tokyo bookstores.*

Middle East
MERIC
2 Bahgat Ali Street, El Masry Towers
Tower D, Apt. 24
Zamalek, Cairo
Egypt
Tel. 20-2-7633824
Fax: 20-2-7369355
Email: mahmoud_fouda@mericonline.com
www.mericonline.com

United Kingdom, Europe
(including Russia and Turkey), **Africa,
and Israel**
The Eurospan Group
c/o Turpin Distribution
Pegasus Drive
Stratton Business Park
Biggleswade, Bedfordshire
SG18 8TQ
United Kingdom
Tel: 44 (0) 1767-604972
Fax: 44 (0) 1767-601640
Email: eurospan@turpin-distribution.com
www.eurospangroup.com/bookstore

**Visit our website at:
www.piie.com
E-mail orders to:
petersonmail@presswarehouse.com**